IT WORKS!

Over 1,000 New Uses for Common Household Items

Mary Ellen Pinkham

#1 *New York Times* Bestselling Author

This book is dedicated to the memory of Benjamin Franklin. The great author, statesman and inventor was as dedicated to practical solutions as I am.

Hello.

As the author of many best-selling helpful hint books and the hostess of HGTV's "TIPcal Mary Ellen," I have built a reputation for quick and easy problem-solving and a very practical approach.

If you've purchased (or are considering purchasing) this book, I suspect that you yourself are a practical sort of person. So in addition to the many alternative uses for everyday things that you'll find within these pages, let me suggest some alternative uses for the book itself.

as a doorstop

to help start your campfire

as a cutting board

to even out a table leg

to line your cat box

to swat flies

to discipline your dog

to dry your shoes

as packing material

to block a draft

to wash windows

as a coaster

as a gift

Of course, I think using a book as a gift is the best idea of all. (My first book became a best seller because so many people did just that.)

While some people like to "say it with flowers," you can be much more creative in sending your message. Package one of the many versatile items I mention in these pages along with a copy of the book and a note such as one found on the the following page.

Jar of pickles	I didn't mean to be a sourpuss.
Sandpaper	Let's just smooth things over.
Toothpicks	I'm so glad we picked each other.
Coffee filters	Life with you isn't the same old grind.
Balloons	You make me fly high.
Coca-Cola	Let's get bubbly together.
Apples	Don't tempt me.
Rubbing alcohol	Sorry if I rubbed you the wrong way.
Plunger	You seemed drained lately.
Garbage bags	Let's start fresh.
Baby powder	Thanks for keeping me calm.
Aluminum foil	Foiled again. Sorry things didn't work out.
Bottled water	You're essential to me.
Salt	I'd like to give you a little pinch.
Can opener	I shouldn't have opened up the discussion.
Duct tape	I'm stuck on you.
Toothpaste	You make me smile.
Rubber gloves	I'll handle you with care.
Fabric softener sheets	Can you soften your position?
Socks	I have met my match.
Shampoo	Don't change a hair for me.
WD-40	Our relationship is like a well-oiled machine.
Lemons	I'd like to give you a squeeze.
Pantyhose	We're in good shape.
Oven cleaner	I do my best work overnight.

I hope you have as much fun with this book as I had preparing it...

Mary Ellen

New Uses for Common
Household Items
A to Z
Have Fun!

ALCOHOL, RUBBING

- Clean away hairspray. Alcohol can make a mirror or a curling iron clean again.

- Make a stainless steel sink shine.

- Remove an ink stain. Sponge the item with rubbing alcohol, then launder as usual.

- Keep alcohol wipes in your pocket or desk drawer for office ink stain emergencies.

- Clean dusty candles. Sponge them with a piece of cotton dampened with rubbing alcohol.

1

- Make the chandelier shine. Spray a chandelier with 1 part alcohol to 3 parts water. Hang an umbrella upside down to catch drips.

- Perfume bottles retain old scent. Before refilling a bottle with a new fragrance, fill it with a capful of rubbing alcohol, shake it, leave it about 1/2 hour, then pour the alcohol out.

ALKA-SELTZER

- Clean a toilet. Drop a few tablets into toilet bowl; wait for 20 minutes, then brush and flush. The citric acid in the product does the job.

- Use as a mouthwash. Alka-Seltzer contains baking soda (which is nature's deodorizer).

- Soothe tired, achy feet. Plop a few Alka-Seltzer tablets into a basin of warm water. Soak feet for at least 15 minutes. (The pain reliever aspirin is the main ingredient in Alka-Seltzer.)

- Eliminate foot odor. Use the soak solution above.

ALUMINUM FOIL

- Remove rust from metal. Scrunch up a few sheets of aluminum foil to do the job.

- When you can't find a pot lid or don't feel like washing one, simply use a sheet of foil as a makeshift lid. The foil will get hot so remove with a pot holder.

- Prevent a pot from burning. If you leave a pot to simmer for a while, make a rope out of foil and wrap it around the burner to elevate the pot slightly.

- Help plants grow. Line the windowsill where plants sit with foil. The foil will reflect the sunlight back into the plants.

- Cut ironing time. Place a large sheet of foil between your ironing board and the cover. The foil absorbs the heat from the iron and reflects the heat into the clothes, so it cuts ironing time in half.

- Keep breads and muffins warm. Line the bottom of a bread basket with aluminum foil and the foil will radiate heat.

- Prevent a pie crust from burning. Place aluminum foil around the edge of the crust before baking.

- Keep celery fresh longer. Wrap it in aluminum foil before refrigerating.

- Make a vegetable cooker for the grill. Line the grill rack with foil and then cut slits into the foil. Place the vegetables on the grill and they won't fall through.

- Prevent the top layer of cheese on a casserole from sticking and burning. Cover the dish with Reynold's Wrap Releaser non-stick aluminum foil. The cheese will be melted perfectly but it won't stick to the foil. Bake casserole uncovered the last 10 minutes.

ALUMINUM FOIL DISPENSER CARTON

- Make a playing card holder for kids. (A waxed paper or plastic wrap dispenser carton would work as well.) Little kids who can't manage to hold a hand of cards can line up the cards in the space between the serrated front of the carton and the carton lid.

ALUMINUM PIE TIN

- Keep campfire pots and pans soot-free. Set them in disposable aluminum pie tins when cooking on a campfire grill.

AMMONIA

- Clean oven racks. Lay them on an old clean towel in the bathtub. Fill the tub with hot water and a cup of ammonia and let set for 30 minutes.

- Remove stains on marble. Mix a few drops of ammonia with hydrogen peroxide. Apply to the stain and let it set for a few hours. Rub with a clean, dry cloth, then wipe off with a damp cloth.

- Take oil paint stains off fabric. Mix 2 T. ammonia and 1 T. turpentine. Rub into stain and rinse. Several applications may be needed.

ANGEL FOOD CAKE PAN

- Make a tip-proof dog dish. Use an angel food cake pan as the dish with a wood stake stuck through the center.

APPLE CORER

- Use as a miniature bulb planter. Plant tiny garden bulbs like galanthus, scilla, and muscari.

APPLES

- Remove odors. Set cut apples on saucers around the home.

ARTISTS' BRUSHES

- Use them as makeup brushes. Buy them at craft stores. They're cheaper than cosmetic brushes and work just as well.

BABY BOTTLE NIPPLE

- Replace a piggy bank plug. Use a rubber baby bottle nipple.

BABY FOOD JARS

- Use as spice holders. Buy the spices in bulk; they're cheaper.

- Organize your nails and screws. For jars with screw on tops, nail the lid underneath a shelf and screw the jar on.

BABY MONITORS

- Use for other family members. Great to keep watch on the elderly, sick and disabled.

BABY OIL

- Johnson's baby oil isn't just for babies. Remove burrs and thorn from your dog. work a little into the tangle, then brush the tangle loose with a brush...etc.

- Remove a bandage painlessly. Pour a small amount of baby oil on the bandage. Work the oil into the bandage before removing it.

- Remove sticky labels. Saturate the label, leave it briefly, then rub it off.

BABY POWDER (see TALCUM POWDER)

- Protect your skin from fiberglass itch. Sprinkle baby powder on exposed skin when working with fiberglass insulation to keep it from sticking.

- Unknot shoelaces. Sprinkle a little baby powder on the knot and it'll be easier to work free.

- Remove grease splatters from clothing. Press baby powder or corn starch onto a powder puff and blot the grease stains until stains are gone.

- Dry-shampoo a pet. Rub the powder in thoroughly, then brush it off. It'll absorb oils and leave your pet smelling like a baby.

- Make rubber gloves easier to put on and off. New rubber gloves have a powdery coating on the inside for this purpose. When the coating wears off, sprinkle your fingers with some baby powder before you put the gloves on.

- Make tight boots easier to slip into. Sprinkle baby powder into them first.

- Clean off quickly at the beach. Sprinkle powder on the wet, sandy spots on your body. When baby powder absorbs moisture, sand brushes off easily.

- Protect your plant bulbs. Dust them with medicated baby powder before planting. Many critters hate the smell and taste of this powder and will stay clear.

- Keep playing cards from sticking. Give them a light dusting of baby powder.

BABY SHAMPOO

- Remove eye makeup. Dilute baby shampoo with water for a gentle remover. Put a few drops on your fingertips, rub on eyelids and wipe off with a damp cloth.

- Make way for seedlings. Add 1 T. of baby shampoo to 1 qt. water and sprinkle over newly planted seeds. This softens the soil and helps the seedlings to push through.

BABY WIPES

- Clean the older kids, too. These are great for wiping kid's noses and dirty faces.

- Clean hands at the gas station. Keep a container in your car to use after filling the tank.

BAG, FROZEN VEGETABLES

- Make a pliable, instant ice-pack.

BAGS, BROWN PAPER

- Remove candle wax from the carpet. Put an unprinted paper bag on the spot, then run a warm iron over it. As soon as the paper absorbs the wax, move a fresh piece of paper onto the stained area and iron again. Repeat until all the wax is absorbed.

BAGS, PLASTIC GROCERY

- Make pompoms for the game. For each one, layer ten plastic grocery bags with handles and flatten to remove air. With scissors, cut 1-inch strips from bottom to top, but do not cut handles. Loop yarn through bag handles and tie tightly at top. Loop yarn around base of bag handles and tie tightly.

- Make a cracked vase usable. Put flowers in a plastic bag filled with water, then put the bag in the vase.

- Reduce paintbrush cleanup. Cover a paint brush with a bag when you go for a break, or even overnight. Make sure the bag is closed tightly and your paint won't dry out.

- Help clean your community. Be a good citizen and carry a few when taking a walk to pick up trash.

- Keep the car clean. Store a few in the car to collect trash.

- Use them for sponge painting. Instead of using an expensive sea sponge, crumple a bag, dip it into paint, and apply it randomly to the wall.

- Treat your feet. Apply a moisturizer to your feet followed by petroleum jelly. Cover your feet with a plastic bag before putting socks on. Wear around the house or to bed (if you can stand it).

- Stop refrigerator drips. Keep raw meat or poultry wrapped in plastic bags to prevent leaking in the fridge.

- Make balloon curtains that really poof. Instead of using tissue paper, stuff lots of plastic bags into the valances. The curtains won't lose their shape.

- Keep Christmas lights organized and tangle-free. Place each string of Christmas lights in its own plastic grocery bag and tie shut.

- Transport a casserole neatly and easily. Put the dish in a doubled set of plastic grocery bags. Center the dish in the bottom of the bags; twist the handles and tie the handles shut. Next, center the plastic-covered dish on a large dish cloth, bringing opposite ends together and tying. To carry, grab the center of both ties. The plastic bag will catch spillovers and the dish cloth will make the dish easy to carry.

- Protect early transplants in the garden. Stake grocery bags over them to protect them from sun, wind, and cold nights.

- Collect weeds or vegetables. Keep a few bags in your garden apron.

- Use them as plant fasteners. Cut into thin strips and use to hold vines and plants in place.

- Keep boots mud-free. When working in a muddy garden, slip plastic-grocery bags over boots or shoes and tie them on securely. The mud won't clump onto the loose plastic as it does onto to shoes or boots.

- Protect a fan. Cover it with a plastic bag when you're putting it away for the season.

- Extend the life of sewing patterns. Spray glue on the tissue pattern pieces and then lay them on plastic shopping bags. You can color code the patterns by using different color bags for each pattern. They will last forever.

- Use as a lint collector. Keep a plastic bag hanging on the door handle of your laundry room.

- Use as a travel laundry bag. Tuck a couple of plastic grocery bags in a suitcase to collect dirty clothes.

- Protect your wipers from the cold. Put plastic bags over your windshield wipers on winter nights and wipers won't be stuck to windshield in the mornings.

- Use as packing material. Anything is better than those messy plastic peanuts.

BAGS, TRASH

- Protect your hiking gear. Place everything inside a tough trash bag, like Hefty Steel bags, seal with duct tape, and then put it in your backpack. Even if the pack falls in a lake, your clothes should stay reasonably dry.

- Use as a garment bag.

- Stuff outdoor chair cushions. Cut trash bags into strips.

- Make a traveling hamper. Use them to hold soiled clothing when you're on the go.

- Aid in replacing cushion covers. After the cover has been washed, put the cushion into a trash bag, then slip it into the cover, open end first. Pull out the plastic bag and the cushion is in place without any tugging.

- Make an emergency raincoat or apron. Just cut arm and head holes, slip the bag over your head.

BAGS, ZIPLOC

- Use as a cosmetic bag. Store toiletries while traveling.

- Use as a purse receipt-holder. Helps with record-keeping. Start a new bag monthly.

- Organize your packing. Pack entire outfits in zipper bags for a child going on a trip. Outfits will always match.

- Store leftover garden seeds. Make sure bag is sealed, and store in a cool, dry place.

- Marinate meat easily. Before freezing meats in freezer bags, pour marinade over the meat, then freeze. When you defrost the meat, it will be marinated and ready to cook.

- Keep game pieces together. Glue a plastic zipper bag to the underside of the box top and store the pieces in it. Everything stays in place, even when the box gets ripped or spills.

- Protect your non-stick pans. Before stacking pans, slide them into plastic zipper bags.

- Shield your cookbook. Slip it into a bag to protect it from cooking splatters.

- Protect the radio at the beach. Dials are accessible even when the radio is tucked into a bag.

- Keep the kitchen TV remote clean. Put it in a plastic bag and if the phone rings you can grab it and click without rinsing off your hands.

- Keep scented candles fragrant. Store them in plastic bags.

- Transport a bouquet. Wrap the ends of the stems with a wet cloth and place the bouquet into a plastic bag.

- Protect carpet during cleaning. Before shampooing carpet, slip clear plastic bags over the furniture legs so they won't stain the carpet.

- Keep the vase clean. Place a plastic bag into a vase, and fill the bag with water. When the flowers are spent, toss 'em, bag and all. No cleanup needed.

- Use as a mixing bowl. Mix scrambled eggs in a plastic bag when camping out.

- Store jigsaw puzzle pieces. Put the bag inside the box, and if the box gets torn, cut out the picture of the completed puzzle and put it in the bag along with the pieces.

- Carry your pills. Put a bag with vitamins and other medication in your purse.

- Keep the phone clean. When your hands are too messy to answer the phone, slip a plastic bag onto your hand.

- Carry baby wipes. Store them in your purse or diaper bag.

- Separate fat in gravy. Pour pan drippings into a bag. Set the bag in a large glass or another container and wait for the fat to rise to the top. Hold the bag up, and snip a small hole in the bottom corner of the bag. After the juices have drained, grab the corner and squeeze it shut before the fat starts to drain.

- Use in the diaper bag. Carry a few to hold soiled clothes and wet/dirty diapers.

- Isolate items in the hamper. Place badly soiled or smelly items in a zipper bag, close the bag and toss in the hamper. Now the whole wash won't be affected.

- Make a lettuce dryer. Punch holes in a large zipper bag and place a few sheets of paper towels in the bag. Place washed lettuce greens inside, close the bag and swing it over your head, helicopter style. As you swing, centrifugal force will push the water out of the bag. Be sure to do this outside.

- Keep a bread crust soft. Place bread in a plastic bag the minute it comes out of the oven or bread maker. Let it set for about 10-15 minutes before removing it from the bag and then wrap in a towel until cool. Once the bread has cooled return the loaf to a plastic bag for storage.

- Soften hardened brown sugar. Put it in a sealed bag with an apple or piece of bread for a couple of days, and the sugar will absorb just enough moisture to soften.

BALLOONS

- Keep a bouquet fresh in transit. Put a little water into a balloon and insert the stems.

- Train the cat. Set a few inflated balloons on a piece of furniture. Once tabby lands on one of them, she won't return.

- Keep a bandage dry. Slip a small balloon over the injured finger when doing dishes.

BAND-AIDS

- Keep a lemon moist. If you need a small amount of lemon juice, poke a small hole in the lemon with a paring knife and squeeze out the desired amount. Cover the hole with a Band-Aid and return to the refrigerator.

- Stop snoring. Adhere a Band-Aid across your nose. This helps open the nasal passages, making breathing easier. If Breathe Right has worked for you, this might work. If it does, you'll save a few bucks.

BAR KEEPER'S FRIEND

- Remove yellow stains from clothing. Make a paste and apply to spots and let set overnight.

BASKETS

- Expand your storage possibilities. Baskets look good, don't cost much, and hold towels, toiletries, board games and magazines. Smaller baskets are great for keys. And instead of a breadbox, cover bread with a basket. A basket will hide anything on your counter. Some are even designed to use upside down.

BASTING SYRINGE

- Suck up a dropped egg.

- Fill a bird's water dish. The baster pokes right through the bars of the cage.

- Degrease a pan. Tilt the frying pan and suck up excess grease when frying bacon or ground beef. Store in a tin can and cool before disposing in the trash.

- Make a perfectly sized pancake. Fill the syringe with pancake batter and squeeze it onto the griddle.

- Drain your lawn mower. A basting syringe is the perfect tool to remove leftover gasoline before you store it for the winter.

- Clean your fish aquarium. For a quick clean up, "vacuum" the bottom of your fish tank with a syringe.

- Change the water in a flower arrangement.

BATH TOWELS

- Make a large, absorbent bath rug. Just stitch together a few large towels.

- Make a bath mitt. Sew two washcloths together.

- Use towels as placemats and napkins for a picnic.

BATHROOM CLEANER

- Get white leather shoes white. Put a few dabs of Comet cleanser cream with bleach on a soft damp cloth and wipe the shoes clean. Wipe off with another clean damp cloth. Now polish as usual.

- Foaming bathroom cleaner will clean a mesh playpen in a jiffy—ideally, outside. Then use soapy water and rinse well.

BATHTUB APPLIQUES

- Patch large holes in screens. Use self-adhesive bathtub appliqués placed back to back. They'll hold, they're water-proof and they'll keep people and birds from walking or flying into the screen.

BAY LEAVES

- Keep bugs out of flour or cereal. Put bay leaves on the shelf. A stick of spearmint gum (wrapped or unwrapped) works great, too.

BED SHEETS

- Make a great tarp for fall leaves. Rake leaves onto an old sheet, fold the corners and drag it to the compost pile.

- Remove a Christmas tree. Lay it on a sheet and wrap around the tree. Carry the tree outside and you won't have to pick up pine needles.

BERRY BASKET

- Arrange flowers. Turn a plastic berry basket upside down and use as a frog.

- Protect bows. Cover gift bows on a package you are mailing with an upside-down berry basket.

BIC PERMANENT MARKERS

- Make plant markers with a Bic permanent marker and plastic knives. Write the name of the seed or flower on the handle and then stick into the soil.

- Re-mark the numbers on oven knobs that are worn off.

- Cover scuff marks on black shoes. Cover it up with a black Bic permanent marker.

- Write prices for a garage sale on a roll of painter's tape with a Bic permanent marker. Tear off each price and apply to the item for sale.

BLACKBOARD ERASER

- Smooth out freshly laid shelf paper.

- Give windows a quick shine.

BLEACH, CLOROX

- Make glasses sparkle. Add a capful of household bleach to the dishwasher.

- Remove coffee and tea stains. Soak cups for a few minutes in a solution of bleach and water.

- Deodorize coolers and thermos bottles with a mild bleach solution.

- Disinfect a garbage pail. Spray a clean pail and let it dry.

- Extend the life of the Halloween jack-o-lantern. Scoop the seeds and pulp out of the pumpkin and swish the insides with 2 T. bleach and 2 c. water. A similar rinse is used by pumpkin growers to cut down on decay.

BLENDER

- Get rid of lumps in gravy.

- Thaw frozen juice in a hurry.

- Turn crackers into crumbs.

- Scramble a large amount of eggs.

- Pulverize dried eggshells (dried in oven on low heat) in the blender and feed to your plants.

- Chop nuts.

BOBBY PINS

- Protect fingers when hammering a nail. Grip the nail between the prongs of the bobby pin.

- Make substitute Christmas tree ornament hangers.

- Replace button on a tufted chair or sofa. Put a bobby pin on the shank of the button, and holding the bobby pin with its ends together, shove the bobby pin into the sofa or chair. The ends will open and the button will stay put.

- Use as a bookmark.

BORAX

- Deodorize carpet. Sprinkle on 20 Mule Team Borax, leave it for an hour, then vacuum.

- Clean hair brushes. Soak them in a basin of warm water, 1 T. dish soap or detergent, and 1/2 c. of borax.

- Remove red wine stain on carpet. But you must act quickly. Add 1 part borax to 3 parts water, and sponge some of the mixture onto the stain. Leave for 1/2 hour, then shampoo the area. After it's dried, vacuum it up.

- Resize a sweater. For a sweater that has shrunk try this solution: Dissolve 1 oz. borax in 2 T. of hot water, add mixture to 1 gal. of lukewarm water, immerse garment, pull gently into shape, and rinse in 1 gal. of warm water to which you have added 2 T. of white vinegar.

BOTTLES (PLASTIC)

- Start a fire. Use an empty squirt bottle as a bellows.

- Use as a dust blower. It's helpful in hard-to-reach places.

- Discard grease and cooking oil. Pour it into a large plastic jug, and when the jug is full, toss it into the trash.

- Make a squirt dispenser for olive oil. A honey bear bottle is perfect.

- Water houseplants. Clean dishwashing liquid bottles with squirt caps are great.

- Line a potted plant. Cut off the bottom half of a large plastic soda bottle and use as a liner for a potted plant. Then use the top as a funnel.

- Store paint. Liquid laundry detergent jugs that have been cleaned thoroughly are ideal for this purpose. Paint is easier to pour, you can work neatly, and the thick plastic handle is superior to those on a regular paint can. Make sure to paint a swatch of color on the front of the jug and write the name of the paint, number, brand and any other important information.

- Use for lawn equipment. Empty shampoo bottles can be used to store oil and to lubricate a lawn mower, a rototiller or other equipment with no fuss.

- Keep wasps away from the picnic table. Cut the top off a two-liter bottle, fill with sugar water, then top with a funnel that fits over the bottle. The sugar water attracts the wasps; they travel through the funnel to get to the water and get trapped.

- Make a safe container for razor blade disposal. Cut a blade-size slit in the side of an empty plastic beverage bottle. Push used blades through the slit so they won't poke dangerously out of the garbage.

- Use for paint or stain application. Transfer stain or paint from a can to a spray or squirt bottle.

BOXES, CARDBOARD

- Keep a leaf bag open and standing straight. Place a 2' x 3' piece of cardboard inside the leaf bag and as you fill the bag with leaves it will not tip over. When the bag is half filled with leaves, remove the cardboard and the bag will stand by itself.

- Make a spray paint booth. The large box that ships a new refrigerator makes the perfect booth to guard the surrounding area when you spray paint a piece of furniture indoors. Cut the box open on one side and stand it up like a room divider. Be sure to protect the floor by covering it with newspaper. Build a small spray booth from a large pizza box. Raise the lids, tape them together at the seams to create a corner and begin painting.

- Use liquor cartons as moving aids. They have dividers that easily separate and organize knickknacks, kitchen utensils, glassware, bathroom supplies, mittens, caps, scarves, etc.

- Make a clutter collector. At the end of the day, put every-thing that's out of place in a cardboard box. When family members are looking for a lost item, tell them to look into the "lost and found" box. Start charging a withdrawal fee and maybe they'll start putting their things away.

- Protect school lunch sandwiches. Slide the sandwiches into empty margarine or butter boxes: they fit perfectly and won't get squished.

- Protect your photographs. Slip photos inside corrugated cardboard light bulbs covers before mailing.

BRACELETS

- Track your daily fruit and vegetable consumption. Here's a neat trick: Start out the day out with nine thin bracelets on your right or left arm. The nine bracelets represent nine daily servings of fruits and veggies. Every time you eat a serving of fruits or veggies, move a bracelet to your other arm.

BRAKE FLUID

- Restore faded blackwall tires. They'll look almost new if rubbed with a thin coat of brake fluid and wiped dry.

BREAD

- Pick up shards of glass. Wad up a slice of bread until it gets sticky, then roll it over the broken glass.

- Use a slice as a spoon rest.

- Fashion a makeshift sink stopper. Ball up a few pieces of soft bread and stick them into the drain.

- Stop flare-ups in the broiler. Place a few pieces of dry bread in the pan to soak up dripping fat.

- Remove excess moisture from a pot of rice. Remove the rice from the heat, place a piece of bread on the top, and cover the pot. In a few minutes, the bread will absorb the excess water.

- Clean a meat grinder. After grinding meat, grind a piece of bread through the meat grinder to remove excess meat.

- Renew the shine on patent leather shoes by rubbing them with a slice of bread.

- Butter corn on the cob. Liberally butter a slice of bread and spin the cob on it.

- Revive hard cookies or soften brown sugar. Place a piece of bread in a jar with the cookies or sugar, seal and leave for a couple of days.

BRICKS

- Crisp a pizza crust. For a brick-oven taste, place two or three clean bricks in a conventional oven and preheat to 400° for 20 minutes. Bake the pizza in a pan on the bricks.

- Improve an inexpensive water sprinkler. Find a cinderblock brick or other kind with holes in it, pull the hose through one of the holes, then attach the hose to the sprinkler. The inexpensive sprinkler will stay in place when watering.

BUCKETS

- Carry your tools and cleaning solution together. Buy a double-sided bucket (two buckets in one).

BUNDT PAN

- Remove corn kernels from the cob neatly. Set the ear of corn on the center hole. When the kernels are cut off, they fall inside the pan and not on the counter.

- Make a tip-proof water dish for the dog. Drive a stake in the lawn and put the bundt pan over it.

BURLAP

- Make a durable wall cover. Your child can tape or pin his favorite painting or posters to burlap and the wall behind won't be damaged.

BUTTER WRAPPERS

- Grease baking pans. Save the wrappers from butter in the freezer, and use them to grease baking and casserole dishes.

BUTTON

- Keep track of pierced earrings. Fasten them to a button.

- Prevent a drawstring from pulling through. Sew a button to each end of a drawstring to keep it from pulling through its casing.

CAN OPENER

- De-vein shrimp with a hook-type can opener.

- Open cardboard boxes. Use a hook-type can opener.

- Open a jar with a sealed lid. Use the tip of the can opener to release a bit of air.

CANDLES

- Keep ink on labels from smearing. Rub a candle over the label.

- Deal with a sticky drawer. Rub the runners with a candle and the drawer will move smoothly.

- Plug a hole. Use a candle stub.

- Seal an envelope. Use a few drops of melted candle wax as a temporary seal on an envelope.

- Use candle stubs as fire starters.

- Keep candles straight. Drip a few drops of melted candle wax into candleholders to hold wobbly candles in place.

CANNING JAR RUBBER SEALS & LIDS

- Keep the cutting board from slipping. Place a few canning jar seals under the board.

- Cook artichokes properly. They'll stand upright if you set each one in a canning jar lid.

CANOE PADDLE

- Use it as a measuring stick. Record the kid's heights as they each grow.

CAR KEYS

- Use as a memory jogger. Put your car keys with the item that you need to remember to take with you.

CARDBOARD TUBES

- Store extension cords. Loop the cord and slide it into a cardboard tube.

- Prevent slacks from creasing. Hang slacks on a paper towel tube that's been slit on one side and slipped over a wire hanger.

- Protect seedlings from cutworms. Push toilet paper tubes into the soil around any seedling that is susceptible.

CARPET SCRAPS

- Use as a stain removal tool. Instead of using a soft brush, try a carpet scrap as the scrubber for removing spots and stains on the carpet, old and new.

- Keep your tote bag in shape. Put a piece of carpet in the bottom of it.

- Keep your boots cozy. Place scraps inside as interlinings.

- Help move heavy objects. Slide a carpet scrap underneath (pile side down), and the object will glide along the floor.

- Clean window screens. Carpet scraps make great brushes.

- Create a garden path. Leftover long strips of carpet make wonderful paths between garden rows. The covering eliminates weeds, and when the garden is wet and muddy you can take a stroll without making a mess.

- Paint the bottom edge of a door. Put some paint on a carpet scrap and open and close the door over the carpet.

- Use as inexpensive floor mats. You may be able to find the perfect size for this purpose at the local carpet store.

- Muffle noise. Put a piece of carpet under a sewing machine or a stereo to cushion the sound of the machine.

CAST-IRON SKILLET

- Keep food from burning. Turn the skillet upside down, place it on a burner, and put your cookpot on top. The pot will heat more evenly so food doesn't stick and scorch, and the consistently lower temperature will reduce the time needed for stirring.

CAT LITTER

- Deodorize stinky shoes. Fill a knee-high nylon stocking with cat litter. Tie shut, place inside shoe and let set overnight.

- Dispose of leftover latex paint. Mix cat litter into the paint can and let it set for a few hours. The cat litter will absorb the paint and can easily be tossed into the trash.

- Remove musty odors from summer homes or cabins. Cat litter in shallow boxes will absorb odors while the house is closed up.

- Keep the garbage pail neat and tidy. Cover the bottom of a trash can with one inch of cat litter to absorb grease and other foodstuff that might leak from the bag.

- Clean up an oil or paint spill. Pour cat litter on the spill for a fast clean-up. A 10-pound bag will absorb about a gallon of liquid.

- Prevent grease fires while barbecuing. Cover the bottom with a one-inch layer of clean, 100% clay, cat litter. Heat coals over the cat litter and grill.

- Get traction on ice or snow. Keep a bag of cat litter in your car for this purpose.

- Make sidewalks and driveways less slippery. Sprinkle the areas with fresh cat litter.

- Deodorize a stale refrigerator. Fill a coffee can with unused cat litter and set it on the middle shelf. Keep the door shut for a week.

- Prevent mold when you store a tent. Fill a knee-high nylon stocking with cat litter, tie shut, then put the stocking into the rolled tent.

- Make a facial masque. Purchase cat box filler that is 100% clay. Combine equal parts litter and water (about 3 T. of each), then process with a mortar and pestle. Apply to clean skin and let dry before rinsing off with warm water. It's a great way to detoxify skin.

- Remove the musty odors from books. Put them in a plastic bag full of cat-box filler, seal and leave for about a week.

CATNIP

- Keep cockroaches at bay. It's surprisingly effective.

CERAMIC TILES

- Make a trivet for hot dishes. Make sure you put a felt pad on the underside to prevent scratching.

- Hide a burn mark. Cover a burn mark on your kitchen counter with a ceramic tile. Use as a permanent hot pad.

CHAIN WEBBING

- Childproof a balcony. Weave chain webbing through balcony railings where openings are dangerously wide.

CHALK

- Prevent tools from rusting. Place a piece of chalk in a toolbox to absorb moisture.

- Prevent tarnishing. Put a piece of chalk in a jewelry box or a silverware chest to stop tarnishing.

- Clean jewelry. Mix a little crushed chalk and white toothpaste together.

- Prevent a screwdriver from slipping. Rub chalk on the end of it.

- Mark the spot for picture to be hung. Instead of using a wet fingertip, use chalk. It won't dry up instantly, and it can be brushed off easily when the job is done.

CHARCOAL BRIQUETTES

- Use as a moisture remover. Fill a coffee can half full and place in a humid closet to absorb moisture.

- Keep tools from rusting. Drop a couple of briquettes in your toolbox.

- Keep rootings fresh. Drop a piece of charcoal in the water in which cuttings are growing to keep them fresh and clean.

- Remove a stump. Each time you cook on a grill, save the leftover hot coals and dump them on the center of a stump. Eventually the stump will be burnt to the ground. (NOTE: Never leave a fire unattended.)

CHECKBOOK REGISTERS

- Record mileage for IRS records. Keep the register in your glove compartment.

CHEESECLOTH

- Make the turkey a self-baster. Cover it with a double layer of cheesecloth that's been soaked with butter, canola or olive oil before roasting. When the turkey is done, remove the cheesecloth for a moist and golden-brown bird. For a crisp, dark-brown bird, remove the cheesecloth half an hour before it's done.

CHERRY PITTER

- Remove pits from olives.

CHOP STICK

- Test the cooking oil temperature. Stick one end of a wooden chopstick into the oil so that it touches the bottom of the pan. If bubbles rise quickly around the chopstick end as it goes into the oil, then the oil is hot enough.

- Use them as tongs. They're great to dig crumbled bread and rolls out of a toaster.

- They're a great tool to fish out paper or other items that might be clogging the toilet. Afterwards, just throw the chopstick away.

CHRISTMAS TREE ORNAMENTS

- Keep the birds clear of tomato plants. Hang red Christmas tree bulbs on tomato plants before the fruit begins to ripen. The birds will peck at the hard ornaments, get frustrated and go away.

CLIPBOARD

- Collect bills on a clipboard. Remove them when they are paid.

CLOTH SCRAPS

- Make a drip catcher. Tie an old rag around your wrist when washing windows and walls. It absorbs the water so it won't run down your arm.

- Quiet a drip from a faucet. Tie an old rag around the spout. It won't fix the leak, but it stops the dripping sound.

CLOTHESPINS

- Make a laundry stain aid. Attach a clothespin to the area that needs attention to remind you to pre-treat a stained piece of clothing,

- Keep the spoon from falling into the pot. Attach a stirring spoon to the cooking pot with a clothespin.

- Create a small wedge or shim. Take a wooden spring-type clothespin apart and use one of the sides for this purpose.

- Make a match holder. Place a match into a clip-type clothespin instead of putting your hands close when you're lighting a fire.

- Seal opened garden seed packets.

- Clip garden gloves together.

- Use as a chip clip.

CLUB SODA

- Deal with pet stains. First, blot up as much of the stain as possible with dry clean white cloths. Then, pour club soda over the stain liberally. Blot up immediately with more clean cloths. Apply a stain remover (following the directions on the bottle) or use equal parts of white vinegar and water. The key to removing any stain is blotting.

COCA-COLA

- Remove rust spots from chrome car bumpers. Use a piece of aluminum foil dipped in cola.

- Clean an aluminum door track. Pour about 1/3 c. of diet cola on the track (regular cola will attract ants), spread it the full length of the track, then wipe with a rag or paper towels. The phosphoric acid does the job.

- Clean a car battery terminal. Pour a can of cola onto it and watch the corrosion bubble away.

- Loosen a rusted bolt. Set a cloth soaked in cola on a rusted bolt for several minutes.

- Clean pennies. Fill a small bowl or glass with cola and drop in tarnished coins. After a few hours, rinse them and wipe them clean.

- Make a moist ham. Wrap the ham in aluminum foil, put it in a baking pan, and pour a can of cola into the pan. Half an hour before the ham is done, remove the foil. Ham drippings mixed with the cola make delicious brown gravy.

- Make a cola fruit salad. Pour cola over a bowl filled with fruit.

- Clean a toilet. Pour a flat can of cola into the toilet bowl and let the "real thing" sit for an hour before flushing.

- Remove road haze from car and truck windshields. A truck driver passed this along. Splash cola on the windshield and let the wipers spread and rub it around. In a minute or so, rinse with windshield wiper spray.

- Clean burnt pots and pans. Boil some cola in the pan and the burnt-on food will come off.

- Remove grease from clothing. Empty a can of cola into a load of greasy laundry. Add detergent and run through entire cycle.

- Remove skunk smell. Sponge yourself down with cola in the shower, then rinse clean.

COFFEE

- Remove garlic odor on hands. Rub them with a teaspoon of coffee grounds and a little water.

- Freshen your breath. Do as the Italians do after eating a meal seasoned with lots of garlic, and chew on a coffee bean.

- Darken faded black cotton. Add extra strong black coffee to the laundry rinse water.

- Kill a headache. Drink a cup of coffee. Caffeine shrinks the blood vessels in your head. In fact many headache medicines contain caffeine.

COFFEE CAN LIDS

- Make trays for sticky foods. The lid catches the drips.

- Separate hamburger patties. Place lids between patties before you put them in the freezer and burgers won't stick together.

- Keep a grapefruit, orange or lemon fresh. Place the cut side down on a plastic lid before storing in the refrigerator.

- Make a drip catcher. When you paint a ceiling, cut a slit in the coffee can lid and slip it over the brush handle.

COFFEE CANS

- Make a safe razor blade disposal unit. Cut a slit in the plastic lid; drop the blade into the can.

- Make round bread. Use a large coffee can. Remove both ends and lay the can on its side in the oven.

- Dispose of grease. Never toss grease down the drain. Instead, put the grease into a coffee can with a lid, put it in a plastic bag, and toss it in the trash.

- Pack supplies for a camping trip. Use a coffee can for items that need to stay dry, like toilet paper, matches, candles, and cameras.

- Carry supplies to the beach. Protect your camera, wallet, keys or any other valuables from water and sand by putting them into a coffee can with a lid.

- Use them as vases. Large cans, especially colorful ones (like yellow and red), make wonderful vases and flowerpots.

- Clean a putty knife. Remove paint globs and stripper from a putty knife by scraping it along the sides of the coffee can.

- Store smelly items in the fridge. Put an opened can of tuna, sauerkraut, dog or cat food into a coffee can with a lid.

- Make storage cubbies in a tool shed or garage. Large clean coffee cans can be nailed to a wall, either upright or turned on their sides.

- Protect newly planted seedlings. In the spring, use coffee cans to cover them at night, then remove the cans during sunny days and when frost is no threat.

- Keep growing squash and melons from rotting. Use cans with lids as perches to keep them off the dirt.

COFFEE CUPS

- Make a makeshift mortar and pestle. Place the ingredients that need to be ground in a heavy stoneware coffee mug and use a heavy glass spice bottle as the pestle.

COFFEE FILTERS

- Make a Popsicle drip catcher. Poke the stick through a coffee filter.

- Keep a cast-iron skillet rust free. Place a coffee filter in it to absorb the moisture. (It's best to keep cast-iron skillets covered with a thin coating of oil.)

- Remove broken cork bits from wine. Strain the wine through a coffee filter.

- Eat neatly. Wrap a taco or a hot dog in a coffee filter.

- Protect your china. Use coffee filters between each dish for padding.

- Line the kitchen scale. Coffee filters hardly weigh anything and will keep the scale clean.

- Line the flower pot. Place a few coffee filters in the bottom to allow water to drain.

COFFEE GRINDER

- Grind hard candy. Toffee or peppermint can be sprinkled on cake frosting.

- Grind herbs and spices.

COINS

- Prevent cookies from burning. Place a coin in each corner of a regular cookie sheet, then place another cookie sheet on top of the coins. You have now created an air-insulated cookie sheet.

- Use as a screwdriver. A dime is very useful.

- Fix a wobbly ceiling fan. Try taping a coin to the top of one of the blades. You might have to move the coin around to different blades until the wobbling problem is solved.

- Check your tires. Insert a penny into the tread. If you can't cover the top of Lincoln's head inside the tread, you need a new tire.

COLANDER

- Make a makeshift vegetable steamer. Put a metal colander in a pan filled with an inch of water.

- Use it as a spaetzle maker. Just turn the colander over and push the spaetzle dough through the holes.

- Guard against spatters. Set the colander over the frying pan, rim side down.

- Eliminate the mess of a new jigsaw puzzle. Open the new box, pour the pieces into a colander and shake. Store the pieces in a bag, and toss out the dust that collected in the colander.

COLORING BOOK

- Find a decorating pattern. You can find something suitable for decorating a cake, making a wall stencil, making an applique, and more.

COMB

- Save your fingers when hammering a nail. Hold a small nail between the teeth of a comb.

- Foil a pickpocket. Fold your wallet over a pocket-sized comb (teeth side up) and keep your wallet in your pocket with the opening facing up. The teeth of the comb will snag on the pocket, making it hard for a thief to remove it easily.

COOKIE CUTTERS

- Decorate a cake. The cookie cutters make good stencils.

COOKIE SHEETS

- Keep a stove clean. Cover burners not in use with a cookie sheet to catch the spattering grease. It's easier to clean a cookie sheet than the burners and drip pans.

- Make oven cleanup easier. Lay a cookie sheet on the bottom of the oven to catch spills.

COOKING OIL

- Remove your makeup. Olive oil does the job for all skin types.

- Cure pet's dry, itchy skin. Add 1 T. of olive oil to your pet's food.

- Prevent cat hairballs. Add 1 t. of cooking oil to one cat's meal daily.

- Soften stiff chamois. Add 1 T. of olive oil to a bowl of water, and soak the chamois.

- Remove tar and oil-based paint.

- Shine a stainless steel sink. Wipe it with a few drops of cooking oil.

- Remove a price label. Saturate it with oil, leave briefly, and rub it off.

COOKING SPRAY

- Stop snoring. Before bedtime, spray a squirt of Pam olive oil cooking spray into a snorer's throat. It lubricates the back of the throat as well as many expensive stop-snoring sprays.

- Make defrosting easier. After you've defrosted and cleaned your refrigerator freezer, spray the bottom and sides with cooking spray. The next time it needs to be defrosted, the ice will fall off in sheets within minutes.

- Prevent dog food from sticking to the dish. Spray it with cooking spray before adding the food.

- Prevent tomato stain on a plastic container. Spray it with cooking spray first.

- Clean up a measuring cup in a jiffy. Coat the inside of a measuring cup with cooking oil spray before adding sticky foods like honey. The ingredients will slip out easily.

- Speed up nail polish drying. Spray it with cooking oil spray.

- Remove bugs from car grills easier. Coat the grill with cooking spray right after car has been washed.

- Keep frosting intact. Spray cooking spray on a sheet of plastic wrap before you cover the frosted cake.

- Prevent food from sticking to foil when cooking. Spray aluminum foil with cooking spray before adding the food.

- Clean up cheese grater fast. Spray it with vegetable oil before using it.

- Keep the string on your power lawn trimmer from breaking or sticking. Coat the line with cooking oil spray.

COOLER

- Insulate groceries that need refrigeration. Keep it in your car to use when you go marketing on a hot summer day.

COOLING RACK

- Mark the bread for even slicing. Cool the homemade bread on its side on a cooling rack. The rack will leave subtle indentations.

- Make a large trivet.

- Store clip earrings on the rungs of a cake cooling rack. Clip them on and they'll be easy to see. Hang the rack with nails. Place a pegboard or snap the "feet" into the grids of a closet organizer.

- Defat the meatloaf. Put the loaf on top of the rack, then put the rack in the cooking pan and fat will drip off as it cooks.

COPPER TUBING

- Repel slugs. Flexible copper tubing from the hardware or home store is much cheaper than copper slug repellent, and it can be shaped to fit snugly around the bases of slug-prone plants.

CORKS

- Clean rusty knives. Just sprinkle some cleanser on the blade and scour the knife with the cork.

- Replace a handle on a pot lid. Set the cork over the lid, then insert a screw from the underneath, up into the cork.

- Lift a hot pot lid without a pot holder. Wedge a cork under the handle of the lid before cooking. The cork will stay cool even when the lid gets hot, making the lid easy to lift off.

CORNSTARCH

- Keep your playing cards from sticking together. Add cards to a paper bag and pour a little cornstarch into the bag. Shake and wipe off the cards with a soft clean rag.

- Shampoo your hair without water. Work a small amount of cornstarch into your hair and brush with a clean brush.

- Make homemade starch. Mix 2 T. of cornstarch with 1 pint of cold water in a clean spray bottle. Shake well before spraying on clothing.

- Clean up a greasy stain. Cover the spill immediately with cornstarch. The cornstarch will absorb most of the spill and make it easy to pre-treat the stain before laundering.

COTTON SWABS, (Q-TIPS)

- Apply glue onto small areas.

- Clean hard-to-reach places. Dip a Q-tip in cleaning solution to clean crevices in car, between telephone buttons or any small area.

- Lubricate small tools and sewing machine parts.

- Apply or remove make up.

CRATES

- Keep the family organized. Place colored plastic crates—a different color for each member of the household—at the door. This works especially well with kids. They can place all school supplies in their crates on returning home from school and return items there, after doing homework or before going to bed, along with anything else needed for the next day. Parents can leave clothes to drop at the cleaner, books to return to the library, etc., in their crates.

CRAYONS

- Cover scratches on furniture. Select a color that matches the furniture and gently rub the crayon over the scratch. Wipe off any excess crayon with a soft dry cloth.

- Re-color spots on clothing that has been damaged with bleach. Select the right color. Iron over the bleach spot with an iron, then color in the spot with the crayon. Cover with wax paper and iron over the wax paper to set the color into the garment.

CREAM OF TARTAR

- Polish your silver. Make a paste with water.

- Clean a burned aluminum pot. Sprinkle cream of tartar into the pan, add a little water and bring to a boil. When the pan has cooled, wash away the debris.

CREDIT CARD

- Use as a scraper. Clean dishes, pots and pans, and use elsewhere when you don't want to scratch a surface. It's nice to have them clean you up rather than clean you out.

CRISCO SHORTENING

- Remove scuff marks on hard surfaces. Apply Crisco to a dry, clean cloth, then rub.

- Polish rubber boots. Rub on clean boots with clean cloths.

CROCKPOT

- Keep mashed potatoes warm. Set the crock pot on low.

CURTAIN ROD

- Keep pot lids tidy. If you store pots and pans in a drawer, install a slender expanding curtain rod in the front of the drawer. Stand the lids up against the rod, and they'll stay in place.

DENTAL FLOSS

- Slice cake layers. Allow the cake to cool and remove it from the pan. Gently saw the cake into the number of layers you want.

- Use instead of thread for beading. Dental floss is strong and more durable than most string.

- Use it to hang a picture.

- Sew with it. Buttons won't fall off as easily when sewn on with dental floss.

- Remove cookies stuck to a cookie sheet. Take a long piece of dental floss and slide it underneath the cookies to loosen them.

- Slice soft cheese.

DENTURE TABLETS

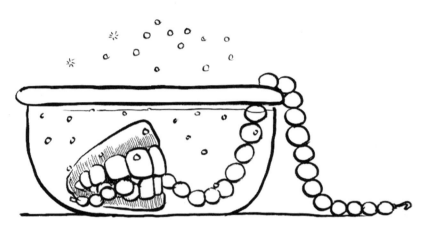

- Clean jewelry. Just drop a tablet into a small bowl of hot water. Add the jewelry and let it set for a few hours.

- Clean a thermos bottle. Fill with hot water and add a tablet. Let it set for a few hours.

- Clean a narrow vase. Fill it with hot water and add tablet. Leave for a few hours.

- Clean a hummingbird feeder. Fill with hot water and drop in a tablet. Leave for a few hours.

DIAPERS, DISPOSABLE

- Mop up a spill. A disposable diaper will quickly absorb liquids from carpets, floor, and elsewhere.

- Water houseplants while on vacation. Soak a diaper in water and lay it on a large tray, then set a pot with a drainage hole on the diaper. Add more water to the tray. The plant will absorb the water as it needs it.

DICE

- Settle arguments. One way to stop those interminable discussions about who gets the next turn is to let the kids throw a set of dice. Decide in advance whether the high or low roller wins.

DISH-DRYING RACK

- Drain vegetables. Cooked corn on the cob and lettuce can drip dry.

- Organize children's coloring books. The silverware holder makes a great place to store pencils, crayons and markers.

- Make a taco holder. The racks can hold tacos while you're filling them.

- Use as a pot lid holder. Store it in a cupboard.

DISHWASHER

- Use it to clean items other than dishes. It can clean sponges, baseball caps, a fan cover and blade, the exhaust fan filter from stove, hubcaps, teething toys and plastic toys, refrigerator shelves and bins, dustpan and brush, dish rack, toothbrushes, candleholders, vases, bathroom accessories, combs and hairbrushes, kitchen exhaust pans, stove knobs and burner pans, kitchen magnets, rattan plate holders, heating vents, some lighting fixtures (top rack only). Keep small items in mesh bags and turn the water temperature down if possible. Air dry only.

- Quickly wash vegetables from the garden. Put them in the dishwasher and run through the rinse hold cycle a few times.

DISHWASHER DETERGENT

- Clean a stained toilet bowl. Add 1/2 c. of Cascade to the toilet bowl and let it set for awhile before brushing the bowl clean with a toilet brush.

- Remove baked-on foods from a pot or casserole dish. Fill the stained pot with hot water and add 2-3 T. of Cascade. Mix and let it set overnight.

- Clean a thin-necked vase. Add 1 t. of Cascade to the vase and fill with hot water. Shake and let set overnight.

- Remove stains on white clothing. Wet the stain with water, then sprinkle on enough Cascade to make a paste. Let it set for a few minutes before brushing it with a soft brush. Once the stain is gone, put the garment through the regular wash.

- Brighten white polyester and remove graying. Mix 1 c. of Cascade and 1 gal. of warm water in a plastic bucket. Soak the dingy clothing overnight, and in the morning run it through the washing machine.

- Remove a nasty concrete stain. Make a paste of Cascade for automatic dishwashers (not the same as liquid dishwashing detergent, for hand washing) and water, and cover the stain. Let it set for a while, then pour hot water on the spot and scrub with a brush. Rinse with hot water.

DISHWASHER RINSING AGENT

- Eliminate streaks when washing your car. Add 1 T. of Jet-Dry to a pail of rinse water.

DISHWASHING LIQUID

- Clean a barbecue grill or oven racks. Do this job outside. Place the grimy grill in a heavy-duty trash bag. Add 1/4 c. dishwashing liquid, 1 c. ammonia and 2 gal. of hot water to the bag, and secure it with a twist tie. Let set for a few hours or overnight. When you open the bag, stand back, because ammonia fumes are powerful. Rinse the grill with a garden hose.

- Clean a dirty narrow-necked vase. Put in a squirt of dish soap, a few tablespoons of uncooked rice and hot water. Shake the vase and let the rice act as an abrasive.

- Wash hair your hair with Palmolive Dishwashing Liquid. It's gentle and works great.

- Use it as a stain remover. Dish soap that is formulated to remove grease from dishes can do the same for your clothing.

- Make your own liquid abrasive solution. Mix together equal parts of dish soap and baking soda.

DOILY

- Recycle as a gift bag. Just thread a ribbon around the doily and pull together to close.

DOOR KNOCKER

- Make a napkin holder to hold down a stack of napkins at an outdoor party or picnic.

DOORS

- Make them into bed headboards.

- Make them into tables.

DRY HAND CLEANER

- Stop bleeding. A few drops of dry hand cleaner will stop the bleeding from a small cut.

- Removes stay on lipstick. Rub Purell Hand Sanitizer over lipstick and wipe off.

DRY MILK

- Add it to your bath. Cleopatra took milk baths, and so can you. Pour 1/2 c. in the tub. The important ingredient is the lactic acid in the milk, which smoothes your skin.

DRYER

- Clean your drapes. Just throw them in the dryer for a few minutes on air only.

- Revive limp gift bows. Throw them in the dryer for a few minutes with a damp washcloth. The combination of heat and moisture will make old bows look almost new.

DUCT TAPE

- Remove a wart. A dermatologist tells me if you cover a wart with duct tape for six weeks, it'll disappear.

- Mend a hole in a tent or a down sleeping bag or jacket.

- Repair an aluminum lawn chair. For a temporary fix, use strips of duct tape (it comes in many colors) in place of ripped webbing.

- Insulate camp cookware. To protect your hands, wrap the handles with a couple of layers of duct tape.

- Fix a football. If the lacing breaks on a leather football, making it hard to grip, place a piece of duct tape over the lace.

- Clean a metal file. Use a piece of duct tape to remove embedded sawdust.

- Repair torn shower curtain ring holes. Tape a piece of duct tape on either side of the hole and then make a new one with a hole punch.

- Prevent a blister. Tape a piece of duct tape on any area of your body that is likely to blister when doing yard work, raking or shoveling.

- Organize a tangle. Tape together any wires, cords, cables that create a mess.

- Protect the floor. Put a strip on the tips of chair legs or the bottom of the rocker to prevent scratching.

- Get the last drop from the bottle. Run a piece of tape along the side of a bottle and tape it to a cupboard upside down. Place a bowl directly underneath it, remove the bottle cap and let the remainder drip into the bowl.

- Close a hole in a pant pocket.

DUSTPAN

- Use as a kitchen tool. A new dustpan can transfer a large amount of chopped food from a cutting board to a pan or wok.

EGG BEATER

- Whip up garden solutions. An eggbeater can blend homemade bug potions and fertilizers.

EGG CARTONS

- Staple the open side of an egg carton to wall, bubble-side out. They make great soundproofers, and you can paint them. (I didn't come up with this one; a college student did.)

- Use for packing. Egg cartons act as shock absorbers for fragile items.

- Store golf balls.

- Store earrings and other jewelry. The compartments keep everything organized. Spray paint the cartons to match the inside of the dresser drawer so it doesn't look like a dresser drawer filled with egg cartons.

- Make a junk drawer organizer. It can hold paper clips, safety pins, thumb tacks and so on.

- Portion out your daily medicine/vitamin dosages.

- Make a taco holder. Tacos set in the grooves of an egg carton will remain upright for easy filling.

- Use as emergency ice cube trays. (Only well-washed Styrofoam cartons should be used for this purpose.)

- Hide your valuables. Put them in an egg carton and store it in the refrigerator.

- Make a fire starter. Place charcoal briquettes in a cardboard egg carton, then light the carton.

- Grow seedlings. Fill the carton with potting soil.

EGG CRATE MATTRESS

- Make a cheap pet bed. Cut a foam egg crate mattress in half (now you have two beds) and cover it with fitted crib sheets.

EGG SLICER

- Slice mushrooms, bananas, strawberries, and kiwi.

ELECTRIC BEATER

- Find a stud in a wall. Plug it in without the beating elements, and use a plastic unit that won't make marks as you drag its flat side along the wall. You'll hear a change in pitch, from a buzzing to a humming sound, and that's where the stud is.

ELECTRIC BLANKET

- Uncurl flooring. Lay a heated blanket on top of resilient flooring that's lying flat.

ELECTRIC BLENDER

- Stop tears when cutting onions. Quarter the onions, place them in the blender and cover with water. Process until the onions are chopped (a few seconds) on a high. Drain water.

ELECTRIC MIXER

- Separate and peel quantities of garlic. With this trick, you won't hesitate to make 40-clove garlic chicken! Press down on the heads of garlic, remove as much of the papery skin as possible, then place them in an electric mixer bowl with the paddle attachment. Mix on low speed until the cloves separate and the peels are removed. The job will be even easier if you oil the mixing bowl lightly.

ELECTRIC RAZOR

- Find a wall stud. Run the razor over the wall and listen for the sound to change. When it does, you've hit the stud.

ELECTRIC TOOTHBRUSH

- Clean your fingernails. Recycle an old electric toothbrush to remove stubborn dirt after gardening. It's much more effective than a scrub brush.

ELMER'S GLUE-ALL

- Remove blackheads. To exfoliate a layer of skin, coat your face with a thin layer of white glue, avoiding your eyes. Let the glue dry, then peel off. Remove any excess with warm water.

- Remove a splinter. Put a drop over a splinter, let it dry, then peel off the dried glue. Hopefully, the splinter will stick to the glue and come out.

- For a doily or any other item you want really stiff, mix 2 parts water and 1 part Elmer's white glue in a bowl. Saturate the item, then squeeze thoroughly before drying on waxed paper.

- Spike your hair. The expensive product in the beauty salon sold for this purpose has white glue as a main ingredient. Just put a teaspoon in a cupped hand, rub your hands together, and comb your fingers through your hair. Comb with a fine tooth comb to remove any excess. It will wash out when you shampoo.

EMBROIDERY HOOPS

- Protect food at a picnic. Enclose plastic wrap with an embroidery hoop and use the "lid" to cover foods when eating outdoors. It's easy to lift on and off.

EMERY BOARD

- Slip-proof new shoes. Rub the soles with an emery board.

- Use as an emergency file.

- Clean dirty pencil eraser.

ENVELOPE

- Improvise kneepads for dirty jobs. Fold padded mailing envelopes in half, then tape them together.

- Use it for a grocery list. Collect all of your coupons in the same envelope.

ERASER

- Make a backing for a post earring. Slice off a disc-shaped piece from a pencil eraser. Make sure the piece is thick enough so it doesn't break apart when you stick the earring through.

- Fix a wobbly table or chair. Glue a piece of an eraser to the bottom of the leg.

- Protect your walls. Glue erasers to the back of a picture frame to prevent it from scratching your walls or tilting sideways.

- Remove surface dirt. A clean soft art gum eraser can remove smudges on cotton upholstery, marks from painted walls, wallpaper and clothing.

- Clean the tracks of a sliding glass door. Wrap a clean damp cloth around the eraser end of a pencil.

ESSENTIAL OILS

- Freshen your footwear. A few drops of essential oil on cotton balls to tuck into your shoes between wearings.

- Make your laundry fragrant. Place drops of oil on a clean, dry washcloth and add it to the dryer with your wet clothes. As the clothes dry, they'll absorb the aroma.

- Scent the vacuum. Moisten a cotton ball with oil and place it in a clean vacuum cleaner bag.

- Freshen the air. Add several drops of oil to a spray bottle filled with water; spritz the air to freshen.

EYE SCREW

- Improvise a corkscrew. Insert an eye-screw into wine bottle cork. Push a screwdriver through the eye of the screw and pull up to remove the cork.

FABRIC SOFTENER, LIQUID

- Prolong the life of pantyhose. Rinse clean pantyhose in a basin of warm water and a dash of fabric softener. Don't rinse, just wring and air dry. The softener will lubricate and soften the fibers, which will help the pantyhose be more resilient and last longer.

- Keep your paintbrushes soft. Rinse them in liquid fabric softener solution.

- Prevent static electricity. Spray diluted fabric softener lightly onto a carpet.

- Make hair conditioner substitute. Mix 1 T. with liquid fabric softener and 2 c. of water. Pour through hair and rinse clean.

- Clean dirty casserole dishes, pots and pans. Fill them with hot water and add a capful of liquid fabric softener. Soak for a few hours and the pan will be easy to clean.

FABRIC SOFTENER SHEETS

- Keep clothing from clinging to pantyhose. Rub a damp used sheet over hose.

- Reduce static electricity. Wipe Venetian blinds and a television screen occasionally with a fabric softener sheet and you won't have to dust as often.

- Repel mosquitoes. Tie a sheet through a belt loop before going outdoors.

- Remove pet hair. Rub the area with a sheet of fabric softener and watch how much pet hair it removes.

- Remove and mask odors.

   Bed: Place a sheet between the mattress and the boxspring.

   Books: Place several sheets throughout the pages of a musty book, then put book in a sealed plastic bag for a few weeks.

   Car: Freshen air by stashing a sheet under the front seat of your car.

   Closet: Hang a few in your closet.

   Clothing: A fabric softener sheet inside mittens and gloves prevents a musty smell when they dry.

   Drawers: Place a few sheets in your clothing drawers.

   Shoes: Shove a sheet in shoes overnight and they'll be smelling sweet in the morning.

   Storage Items: Drop a sheet inside.

   Suitcase: Before storing your suitcase, drop in a sheet or two.

- Remove baked-on foods. Just put a fresh fabric softener sheet in the dirty pot, fill with hot water and let it set overnight. The anti-static agent in fabric softener sheets weakens the bond between the food and the pan while the softening agents soften the baked-on food.

- Clean cobwebs from ceilings and hard-to-reach corners: Put an old sock on the end of a broom handle or PVC pipe (great for vaulted ceilings). Wrap several sheets of used fabric softener sheets around the sock and fasten with a rubber band.

- Use as an emergency furniture duster. Put a few used sheets together and dust away.

FAN

- Dry hand-washed dishes and clothing quickly. Put them in front of a fan.

- Minimize kitchen odors. When cooking foods such as fish, sauerkraut and cabbage, aim the fan out the window

- Cool cakes, cookies and brownies.

- Speed-dry a recently painted room, a damp carpet, or a wet mattress.

- Create white noise. When traveling, carry a small portable fan to drown out other sounds and help you sleep.

- Banish mosquitoes. They hate windy areas. Place a large fan on a porch or deck and run it on high.

FEBREZE

- Eliminate odor in shoes and sneakers. Spray the inside of each shoe with Febreze.

FILM CANISTERS

- Prepare the food processing mixer bowl for soaking. Set an old 35mm film canister over the hole so you can fill the bowl with water.

- Store leftover garden seeds.

- Make eyes for a snowman.

- Prepare an emergency sewing kit to stow in your purse. Include needles already threaded with black and white thread, small shirt buttons, and safety pins.

- Hide a house key.

- Store buttons, screws, nails, pins, paper clips, and more.

FISHING LINE

- Remove dealer stickers. If a sticker is applied with double-sided tape (and not with a screw), hold the fishing line tightly, then run it under the sticker. Make a sawing motion as you pull the line through the adhesive until the sticker falls off. Remove any leftover adhesive by spraying with a household lubricant such as WD-40 and rubbing vigorously. You may need several applications to remove the adhesive completely.

FISHNET

- Use it as a wall covering. Attach items with clothespins (which come in many fun colors).

FLASHLIGHT

- Light up a Halloween pumpkin. Less messy, safer than candles.

FLEXIBLE CUTTING MATS

- Put cutlets between them to pound the cutlets thin. They're sturdier than waxed paper.

FLOUR

- Help in fertilizing your lawn. If you mix a little flour in with the dry fertilizer, you'll be able to see exactly where the fertilizer has been spread and identify areas you missed.

- Coat nuts and raisins before you add them to a recipe. The nuts won't sink to the bottom.

FOOD COLORING

- Distinguish cooked eggs from hard-boiled ones. Add food coloring to the water when you're hard-boiling eggs. From the dyed shells, you'll know at a glance which are which.

FRAMES

- Protect recipes while cooking. Slide a recipe into a Plexiglas frame and set it on the kitchen counter.

FREEZER

- Stash a waiting-to-be-ironed garment. It will be easier to iron and it won't mildew.

- Deodorize shoes. Leave them in the freezer overnight to kill bacteria.

- Remove leftover candle wax. Put a votive candle in the freezer. When the candle wax is frozen it will pop right out of the holder.

- Make soft cheese easier to grate. Put the cheese in the freezer for a while.

FRENCH DOORS

- Hinge two together and use them as a room-dividing screen. They define the area but let light through.

FROZEN JUICE

- Make an emergency ice pack. Wrap a dish cloth around a can of frozen juice.

FURNITURE POLISH

- Make a three-ring notebook open smoothly. Spray a bit of Pledge on a soft dry cloth and polish the metal rings. Pages will slide more easily.

GARBAGE PAILS

- Get night tables and extra storage all in one. Buy 40-gallon pails, either plastic or metal: have a round, plywood top made; and cover with a circular cloth that hangs to the floor. For an extra touch, have a glass cover made as well.

GARDEN HOSE

- Carry a heavy bucket with ease. Cut a short piece of garden hose. Make a lengthwise slit and then slip it over the handle of the bucket.

- Protect your hands when raking. Slip a piece of hose over the rake handle.

- Keep electrical cords safely out of the way. Cut a short length of old garden hose and slit it lengthwise on a diagonal. Spread open the cut hose and tack it into the wall or ceiling. Now push the cord through the slit until it moves freely.

GARDEN HOSE CONTAINERS

- Place attractive weed baskets around the garden. Lightweight garden hose containers or garden pots are just the place to toss the weeds.

GARDEN PUMP SPRAYER

- Blow up birthday party balloons in seconds. Slide the balloon over the nozzle of a clean garden pump sprayer and pump.

GARDEN WATER SPRINKLER

- Clean underneath your car. Say goodbye to winter's residue of salt and other debris in spring when you put a sprinkler under the car and let it run for about 15 minutes.

GARLIC

- Repair a hairline crack in a vase. Rub a clove of garlic over the crack. Once dry, the vase should not leak. (And it will keep vampires away.)

- Help keep a dog or cat pest-free. Add a touch of garlic juice to the pet's drinking water.

- Ward off many common insects. Tuck a clove of garlic into the pot of a houseplant. Or use liquid garlic and cayenne pepper. The former is sold as a pest repellent at garden stores, and a cayenne pepper formula is also available to keep critters from eating your plants and flowers.

GARMENT BAG

- Store long rolls of wrapping paper. Hang them in a garment bag, then hang it a closet.

GELATIN

- Help whipped cream keep its shape. Mix 1 t. of Knox gelatin in 2 T. hot boiling water until dissolved. Then add to 1 c. of heavy cream and whip.

- Make a starch substitute for delicate fabrics. Dissolve one packet of unflavored Knox gelatin in 2 quarts of hot water.

- Crisp the curtains. Instead of starching them, dissolve 1 packet of unflavored gelatin in 2 quarts of hot water and add to the final rinse water.

GLOVES, PLAYTEX

- Punch up the Halloween punch. Turn a new, clean glove inside out, fill it with green colored water, and freeze. Then cut and strip the glove from the frozen hand and slide it into your bowl. Eeeeyeww!

- Keep broom in place. Slip a cut-off glove finger onto the top of a broom handle and the broom won't fall when it's leaning against a wall.

- Make a grip for hand or garden tools. Use a finger cut from a rubber glove.

- Flip through paperwork easily. Wear a rubber glove finger on your index finger.

- Make heavy-duty rubber bands. At the wrist end of an old glove, cut strips.

- Make finger puppets for the kids. Glue yarn onto the rubber fingertips for hair and draw faces with permanent markers.

- Prevent curtains from snagging on the rod. Place a rubber finger over the tip.

- Remove pet hair. Dampen gloves and rub them across your upholstered furniture.

- Protect your hands not only when you're cleaning or washing dishes. Gloves can keep your hands covered when you clean the bird or hamster cage, remove fish from a hook, scale or clean it, change a car tire or check the oil dipstick, clean the cat litter box, tie dye clothing, apply pesticides, chop hot peppers, paint or stain, bathe a pet, change a diaper, work with insulation, dye Easter eggs, clean a fireplace, dress game, clean the oven, shuck oysters, pick over shellfish, remove a bug, or change ink cartridges.

- Make a Thanksgiving puppet. Color the fingers with permanent markers for colorful feathers.

- Get a grip. All these jobs are easier when you wear a rubber glove: removing a tight jar lid, lifting a heavy roast from the pan, unscrewing a light bulb, rowing a boat, holding a card hand.

GLOVES, WORK

- Polish chair rungs. Slip on a flannel-type work glove and spritz with furniture polish to quickly clean the rungs of wooden chairs.

- Apply stain. Use white cotton utility gloves pulled on over rubber gloves. They give you better control than a brush.

GOLF BAG

- Store rakes, hoes, and other garden equipment.

GOLF TEES

- Mark where you've planted garden bulbs.

GRAPEFRUIT

- Smooth rough and dry elbows. Cut the fruit in half and rub your elbows in a circular motion, then rinse. The citric acid is a great exfoliator.

GRAPEFRUIT KNIVES

- Transplant seedlings.

- Weed a lawn.

GRAPEFRUIT RINDS

- Trap garden slugs. Leave grapefruit and melon rinds in your yard each evening. Scrape the collected slugs into soapy water the next morning. You'll need fresh rinds every few days.

- Brew the rind in water to make a "tea." Add honey and a little brandy for an excellent cold remedy. It supplies vitamin C and quinine.

GRATER

- Grate egg yolks with a Mouli grater.

GREETING CARDS

- Recycle as postcards. Cut off the back.

GUTTER DOWNSPOUT

- Add storage space in the garage. Mount a two-foot length of gutter downspout on the wall and drop in dowels and molding strips.

HAIR CONDITIONER

- Stretch a shrunken wool sweater. Let the sweater soak in a sinkful of water and half a cup of conditioner. Not guaranteed, but fibers may "relax" enough so you can reblock the sweater to its original, larger shape.

HAIR DRYER

- Loosen a snapshot stuck in a magnetic photo album. Blow warm air underneath the plastic page and remove the photo gently.

- Deal with a drawer that's sticking. Remove the drawer and its contents or, if you can't, remove drawers near it. Aim a blow dryer set at medium at the drawer several inches from the wood. For a few minutes, move it back and forth along the drawer length. Once it's open, rub a bar of soap or candle on wood runners, or spray with furniture polish or non-stick vegetable spray. If runners are metal, use a light lubricant.

- Defog a bathroom mirror.

- Thaw a window or a car door lock that is frozen shut.

- Dry the inside of rubber gloves.

- Set the icing on a cake.

- Unclog a jammed automatic ice maker.

- Restore the shape of a wrinkled bow.

- Remove candle wax from furniture or wallpaper. Soften the wax with the dryer, set to medium and held 6-8" away, then use a plastic scraper (or credit card) to scrape away the excess.

- Loosen shelf paper, stickers, and decals.

- Remove wrinkles from a plastic shower curtain or table-cloth. Just point the hair dryer at the item.

- Make bandage removal less painful. Soften the adhesive from a bandage with a hair blower and it will be easier to pull off.

- Shrink-wrap plastic around any object.

- Dry salt and pepper shakers after washing. Then there will be no moisture to cause lumping.

- Determine which windows are leaking heat. Have someone hold a lit candle just inside a window while you blow air along the outside window frame. If the flame flickers, you'll know where to caulk.

- Warm up the bed.

- Speed-dry joint compound or anything else.

- If you have down-drafting while trying to light a fireplace, blow the dryer (set on hot) up the chimney flue to start the cold air rising.

HAIR SHAMPOO

- Use as liquid hand soap. The ones with conditioner are especially kind to hands.

- Spot clean natural fiber rugs or upholstery.

- Remove grease stains from clothing.

- Make a substitute for shaving cream. Mix equal parts of conditioner and shampoo. (Good way to use up excess of these items.)

- Make wool sweaters less itchy. Wash them with shampoo, rinse with a hair conditioner.

- Wash your horse's hair. Horses love getting a "people" shampoo and it costs less, too. The purple formula meant to whiten hair works wonderfully on red and white paint horses.

- Wash your dog. First shampoo your pet with doggy shampoo, then follow with yours. Your pet won't smell dog-like afterwards.

- Pre-treat collar ring before laundering.

- Hand wash pantyhose.

- Clean and polish virtually every hard surface. Mix a little shampoo with baking soda.

- Clean fiberglass sinks and tubs.

- Clean combs and brushes.

- Use as shower gel. Herbal shampoos smell wonderful and cost only a fraction of the gels. In Europe they market shower gels as all-in-one body and hair cleaners.

- Protect your swim mask from fogging. Divers and snorkelers put a drop of baby shampoo on the lenses of their diving masks to keep them fog-free. Rub one drop on the inside of each lens and rinse briefly in salt water, and you're good to go!

- Clean craft paint brushes. Use a few drops of shampoo without conditioners on a plate. Swish the brushes vigorously in the shampoo, then rinse and repeat until all the paint is gone. The cheaper the shampoo, the better.

HAIRSPRAY

- Thread a needle easily. Spray the end of the thread with hairspray to stiffen it.

- Remove ink stains. Use inexpensive, oil-free hairspray like Aqua Net.

- Keep chalk art from smearing or fading. Cover with a coat of (inexpensive, oil-free) hairspray. Not for ink drawings: hairspray will make it run.

- Deal with a zipper that comes unzipped. Sprayed with hairspray containing lacquer. It may stay in place. (Note: Cover the fabric surrounding the zipper before spraying.) If not, put a button at the top of the zipper and fasten an elastic loop to the zipper to hook onto it.

- Repair frayed, satin-covered Christmas ornaments. Smooth down the loose threads and give the ornament a shot of (inexpensive, oil-free) hairspray to keep the threads in place.

- Keep shoelaces tied. Spritz some hairspray on the laces before you tie them.

- Stop a pantyhose run. Give it a shot of Aqua Net.

- Stiffen ruffles on curtains. Give them a shot of (inexpensive, oil-free) hairspray.

- Give recipe cards a protective coating.

- Recycle Sunday's cartoon section as wrapping paper, but spray it with hairspray before use so it won't smear.

- Preserve autumn leaves.

- Get rid of an annoying flying bug. Hairspray will stop it in its tracks.

HAMPER

- Make a night table out of a clothes hamper. Have a round plywood top made, and cover with a circular cloth that hangs to the floor. For an extra touch, have a glass cover made as well.

HAND GEL

- Clean tarnished silver. Squirt a little antibacterial hand gel on a clean cloth and polish away.

HANGERS, MULTISKIRT

- Keep tablecloths, napkins or placemats organized on hangers.

- Hangers can also hold scarves.

HANGERS, PANT

- Keep the cookbook open. Clip it with a pants hanger and hang on the cupboard door.

- Hang a large washed rug on a clothesline. Clothespins aren't strong enough for such a heavy item, so clip two or three pant hangers to the rug, and then hang it.

HANGERS, WIRE

- Eliminate static electricity. Rub a wire hanger between yourself and the clinging clothing. If Joan Crawford had known this, she would have LOVED wire hangers.

- Dry wet tennis shoes. Pull up on each side of a wire hanger and you've got the perfect place to hang them. Put the hanger on the shower rod.

- Make a towel holder for camping or working outdoors. Cut the wire hanger in the middle, then slip it on a roll of paper towels.

- Dry a paintbrush that's just been cleaned. Turn a hanger upside down, and hang the paintbrush on the hanger hook.

- Hold the drapes aside when you're vacuuming. Slip the ends through a hanger and hang it on the curtain rod or valance or other convenient spot.

- Make skewers to roast hot dogs and marshmallows. Just cut and straighten out the hanger.

- Make a holder for cleaning paintbrushes. Good brushes lose their shape as a result of setting on the bottom of paint thinner container. So cut the hanger, bend it around the threads of a canning jar that contains paint thinner, then bend the hanger properly. The brush will hang without touching the bottom of the jar.

- Make a giant-size bubble blower. Unwind a wire hanger and bend one end of the hanger into a circle. Pour a bubble solution (dish soap and water) onto a cookie sheet, dip the hanger, and pull slowly through the air.

- Make a bookend. Snip off the hook of a hanger with wire cutters and then bend it into a 90-degree angle. Slide one end under the books, and use the other end to hold them up.

- Keep flowers from falling over in your garden. Use a straightened wire hanger as a stake. Form a loop at one end and the flower can grow right up through it.

- Restore sucking power to your vacuum. Unwind a wire hanger, bend one end into a hook, and use it to clean out the vacuum hose.

HANGING PLANT CONTAINER

- Use as a clothespin holder. When it hangs on the clothesline, rainwater will drain through the drainage holes.

HERBS AND SPICES

- Bay leaf: Keep pests out of flour and other dried goods. Add a bay leaf to the top of the bag.

- Cayenne pepper: Keep critters out of the trash. Sprinkle cayenne pepper on the lid of an outdoor garage can.

- Cloves: Use as a sachet. Place cloves in cheesecloth and tie it closed.

- Cream of Tartar: Brighten handkerchiefs or doilies. Make a solution of 1 gal. warm water, 1 T. of cream of tartar and a small amount of laundry detergent. Soak the item for a while, and then launder it as usual.

HYDROGEN PEROXIDE (3% SOLUTION)

- Sterilize a toothbrush. Soak it in hydrogen peroxide.

- Remove a blood stain. Nurses know this trick. Pour a bit of the peroxide on the stain and let it bubble up. Then rinse the spot with cold water. Repeat the process until the stain has mostly faded or disappeared altogether, and then launder as usual.

- Remove rust spots on laminates. Make a paste of hydrogen peroxide and cream of tartar or baking soda. Apply to the rust spot and let stand for 30 minutes. Scrub with a sponge and rinse.

- Disinfect fruits and vegetables. Add 1 T. per gal. of water. Soak fruits or veggies in solution for 10 minutes. Drain, then soak in clean water for 15 minutes.

- Remove perspiration stains. Mix equal parts of cold water and hydrogen peroxide. Apply and let stand for 30 minutes. Launder as usual. Do not use on wool, silk or fabrics that must be dry cleaned. If the perspiration has damaged the fibers in the fabric, however, this won't work.

- Whiten old white tennis shoes. Rub full-strength hydrogen peroxide on dirty tennis shoes and let them dry in the sun.

ICE BUCKET

- Keep food hot. Transport and/or serve it in an insulated ice bucket.

ICE CREAM SCOOP

- Form uniform muffins. Use the scoop to portion out the batter into the tin.

- Form uniform burger patties. Scoop up a portion of meat, then flatten it out with the palm of your hand or bottom of a glass.

ICE CREAM STICKS

- Use as garden stakes.

- Identify paint in cans. Dip in paint and tape to the can so you can see the color for future reference.

- Use to frost holiday cookies. Sticks can stir various colors of frosting, too.

ICE CUBE TRAYS

- Start seedlings. Just punch a few drainage holes in the bottom of the tray with a hammer and nail. This is especially helpful for large seeds.

- Freeze small quantities of foods. Beef or chicken stock, tomato paste, or leftover coffee, wine, or tea can be frozen, transferred to plastic bags, and added in the amount needed without any need for opening or defrosting a large container. Coffee or tea cubes are great to add to iced coffee or tea.

- Freeze leftover egg whites. Freeze one egg white per segment. Frozen egg whites will keep for a year.

ICE CUBES

- Remove a dent in carpet. Drop an ice cube on the spot and let it melt. Blot up the excess water and the indentation will pop up.

- Mix salad dressing. To help vinegar and oil mix, drop an ice cube into bottle, then close the lid and shake well. The ice helps the ingredients emulsify.

- Help a child get the medicine down. Sucking an ice cube before taking bad-tasting medicine helps, because the ice will temporarily numb the taste buds.

- Revive a loaf of stale bread. Rub an ice cube (or drizzle water) across a loaf of unsliced bread until the crust is damp, then bake at 350° for 10-15 minutes or zap in the microwave.

- Water a Christmas tree with no spills. Add ice cubes to the water container.

- Remove a splinter painlessly. Numb the area with ice before extracting it.

- Reheat leftover rice and keep it moist. When you warm it in the microwave, put an ice cube on top.

ID CARD

- Make a weatherproof tag for tools, etc. Take an expired credit card, trim off the identifying number, and leave only your name and enough surface to punch a hole.

- Use as a scraper. Good to scrape dough off counter or board, or to scrape anything off a surface, such as glass or enamel, that might scratch.

IODINE

- Conceal scratches on dark wood.

IRISH SPRING SOAP

- Keep the deer away. First, drill numerous small holes all around 35 mm film canisters, fasten them to the top of short wooden stakes with screws, and fill the canisters with chunks of this soap. It's very effective as a deer deterrent. Just enough of the strong scent of the soap penetrates through the holes to keep the deer from munching. Place the stakes 15 to 20 feet apart and hidden behind plants where possible.

IRON, STEAM

- Repair a dent in wood furniture. Place a damp cloth over the dent. Set the iron on medium and hold it on the cloth for a few minutes or until the cloth has dried. Dampen it again, and continue this procedure until the dent is gone.

- Plump up a carpet "dent" when heavy furniture as been removed. Lay a damp cloth on area and gently press with a hot iron.

IRON GATES

- Use as a bed headboard.

- Mount as a hanging pot and pan rack.

- Make into a screen for your fireplace.

IRONING BOARD

- Use as a substitute for extra counter space.

- Use as a makeshift bar.

- Make a tray table for someone confined to bed.

IVORY SOAP

- Relieve a mosquito bite itch. Rub with a wet bar of Ivory soap and let it dry. The itch should be gone.

- Keep fingernails clean when gardening. Scrape fingernails over a bar of soap before putting on garden gloves.

JARS

- Use as a corn butterer for picnics: Fill a clean mayonnaise jar half full with hot water. Pour a stick of melted butter into the jar. The butter will rise to the top. Dip a corncob into the jar, and when you lift it back out, the cob will be coated with butter.

KETCHUP

- Clean tarnished silver. Squirt a little ketchup on a soft cloth and rub the tarnish off the silver. If the item is heavily tarnished, cover the item with ketchup and let it set for no longer than 15 minutes. This works because ketchup is acidic—acidic enough to ruin a tarnished item if you leave it too long. So take care. This tip appeared in my first book in 1979 and it's still a favorite.

KITCHEN TIME

- Discipline the kids. End quarrels with the kids about whose turn it is—says that when the timer rings...whose turn it is. You can also sound a bed-time warning and set a limit on dressing/undressing time.

KNIVES

- Check whether pasta is done. Use a serrated knife to pull out just one strand of spaghetti.

- Make an emergency dish rack. Set the cups or glasses on butter knives or chopsticks that have been lined up in a parallel line about two inches apart on a dish towel. The excess water will drain onto the dishtowel and air will be able to get under the glasses and dry quickly.

KOOL-AID

- Make your cheeks glow. Cherry Kool-Aid can be used as emergency blusher.

- Fix hair that's turned green in the pool. Make a paste of banana-flavored Kool-Aid and water. Rub the mixture through your hair to remove the green. Rinse thoroughly.

KRAZY GLUE

- Make nail wrap. Cut a piece the size of your fingernail from a coffee filter and use a drop of Krazy Glue to fasten it to your nail.

LADDER

- Make a trellis for climbing plants.

- Organize the herb garden. Lay the ladder on the ground, fill the spaces with soil and plant the different herbs in each section.

- Add counter space for a party. Place a board between two ladders. The remaining steps can be used to store other items.

- Hang pots and pans. Suspend a small painted section of a ladder from a ceiling with rope, chain or wire.

- Keep tricycles out of the street. Lay an extension ladder across the driveway.

- Use when painting shutters. Lay a 2 x 4 between two step ladders. Hook a wire clothes hanger through the top louver of the shutter and slip the hanger over the 2 x 4. You can paint all sides and edges without having to touch the shutter, and it makes the perfect drying rack.

LAUNDRY BASKET

- Make a grocery carrier. Keep one in the trunk of your car for this purpose.
- Keep garden hoses and long heavy-duty electrical cords neat. Store them in a round laundry basket.

LAUNDRY DETERGENT

- Clean whitewall tires. Scrub with a stiff clean brush and undiluted liquid Tide with Bleach.

LEAF BAG

- Use as a moving aid. Heavy-duty leaf bags are roomy and heavy enough to hold a load; they can be written on; and they're easily collapsed and stored for reuse.

LEAF BLOWER

- Use as a dusting aid. A small leaf blower can be used under heavy beds, sofa, refrigerator and under your car seat. You can also blow away cobwebs from ceilings and walls, especially where you can't reach, then vacuum up the dust. I use this tip every spring when we open up our cabin in northern Minnesota.

LEAF SHINE

- Shine your straw hats with leaf shine for plants.

LEATHER PURSE

- Use for patching. Cut it up and sew patches on knees and elbows.

LEMONS

- Dry up pimples quickly. Dab them with lemon juice a few times daily.

- Smooth out elbows. Make a paste of lemon juice and baking soda and rub.

- Clean grimy fingernails. Twist them into half a lemon, then clean them with soap and water.

- Remove grease on barbecue grills. Rub the grill with a cut lemon.

- Remove rust marks. Rub the stain with half a lemon.

- Clean the bottom of copper pots. Sprinkle salt on a half a lemon and scrub the pot.

- Whiten tennis shoes. Spray them with lemon juice and put them in the sun.

- Neutralize the harsh smell of vinegar cleaning solutions. Twist a few lemon peels and add them to the cleaning solution.

- Whole lemons look great stacked in a clean glass filled with daisies. The lemons will act as a frog and anchor the flowers.

- Keep fish from sticking to the barbecue grill. Put lemon slices underneath it while you cook it.

- Cut the smell of cooking cabbage. Place half a lemon in the cooking water.

- Keep mushrooms white and firm when sautéing. Add a teaspoon of lemon juice to the melting butter.

- Clean your greasy fingers. Use lemon slices and a wet rag to clean your fingers when eating barbecue ribs and chicken.

- Turn pages or count money quickly. Dip your finger into half a lemon to cut the natural oils that might slow you down. My local supermarket cashier does this.

- Keep cut fruit from darkening. Store a small spray bottle of lemon juice in the refrigerator for this purpose.

- Cut down on soap film and neutralize odors when bathing a dog. Add a few drops of lemon juice to the rinse water.

- Whiten socks. Soak them in hot water and 2-3 T. of lemon juice.

LETTUCE

- Keep reheated food moist. Cover leftovers with a few lettuce leaves before you microwave them. The food doesn't dry out and remains flavorful.

LIGHT BULB COVERS

- Protect photos in the mail. Save the corrugated cardboard light bulb covers and slip your photographs inside so they won't get bent.

LIP BALM

- Prevent a light bulb from sticking. Coat the threads on a light bulb with ChapStick before screwing it into a socket. This will make removal easy.

- Make a zipper glide. Rub some along the teeth.

- Make a candle easy to remove. Coat the inside of a candle-holder with lip balm.

- Moisturize cuticles and elbows.

- Keep bushy eyebrows in place.

- Protect skin when dyeing hair. Before you start, rub lip balm along your hairline so it doesn't discolor.

- Get a tight ring off your finger. Coat it with lip balm.

- Make drawers and windows glide easier. Rub the tracks with ChapStick.

- Protect yourself from windburn. Rub some ChapStick on your face.

- Help screws and nails penetrate wood easily. Rub them with ChapStick.

LIQUID DIAL

- Clean chopping blocks. It has germ-killing ingredients.

- Clean your eyeglasses.

LOOFAH GLOVES

- Slip them on to clean the bathroom. Dip your hands in a little cleansing agent and you can clean showers, bath and countertops in a jiffy.

- Wear them to scrub potato skins clean.

LUBRICANT

- Keep boots clean. Spray a lubricant on them before you work in a muddy yard. Water will easily rinse the boots off.

LUGGAGE CARRIER

- Bring it along when you go Christmas shopping. Best choice: the kind that folds down and has an elastic cord to hold the luggage.

LYSOL DISINFECTANT SPRAY

- Remove musty odor from a book. Fan open the pages and stand the book before a small fan. Spray Lysol from behind the fan, so it scatters onto the pages. (Not for valuable books.)

MAGNETIC KNIFE RACK

- Use it in the medicine cabinet. It will hold tweezers, scissors, etc.

- Mount it near the workbench. It can hold screwdrivers, pliers, and other tools.

MAPLE SYRUP

- Get rid of wasps and bees while picnicking. Coat a few pieces of cardboard with maple syrup and place at a distance from the picnic table. The pests will be attracted to the sugary sticky treat and get stuck in it.

- Divert ants. Mix 4 T. maple or corn syrup with 1 t. borax. Pour a dab of the mixture into small, lidded plastic containers. Poke holes in the lid large enough for the ants to enter. Set the covered containers in areas frequented by ants.

MARBLES

- Get the last drops of fluid out of the spray bottle. Drop a few marbles in to raise the level. (You can do this with costly perfumes, too. Substitute aquarium glass for marbles.)

- Use them decoratively in a vase. Add them to real or silk flowers for added color at the base or as a frog to keep flowers in position.

- Have them remind you the water's boiled away. Place a few marbles in the bottom of a double boiler. When you hear them rattle, you'll know it's time to add water.

MARGARINE BOXES

- Protect school lunch sandwiches. Slide them into an empty box. They fit perfectly and won't get squished.

MARGARINE TUBS

- Make traps for houseplant pests. Cut bright yellow margarine tubs into small rectangles and coat with petroleum jelly. Attach to a small stake and insert into a houseplant to attract aphids and white flies.

MARSHMALLOWS

- Protect the frosting when transporting a cake. Place miniature marshmallows on toothpick tips. Insert the toothpicks into the cake and lay the plastic wrap over the marshmallows.

MATCHBOOKS

- Use them as a memory jogger. Carry a book of matches from the hotel where you're staying. If you forget the address, check the matchbook. (Just don't forget why you're carrying matches when you gave up smoking years ago.)

MAYONNAISE

- Remove a white ring from furniture. Rub mayonnaise and cigarette ashes into the spot. Rub until the spot blends in with the undamaged part. Work very gently with a clean, dry cloth, and treat only the top layer. Polish when you're done.

MEASURING CUPS

- Use stainless steel measuring cups as mini saucepans. Placed over the stove burner, they can hold and heat small amounts of butter or other sauces.

MEAT TENDERIZER

- Relieve a bee or wasp sting. Once the stinger has been removed, make a paste of meat tenderizer and water and apply to the area. The enzymes in the meat tenderizer break down proteins in bee venom.

MELON BALLER

- Core apples and pears.

MESH DISH SCRUBBER

- Keep flatware in place in the dishwasher. If knives fall out of your utensil basket, place a mesh dish scrubber in the bottom of the basket to keep objects from falling through the slats.

METAL WIRE SIEVE

- Make a great vegetable or shellfish steamer. The sieve is easy to use because of the handle.

MICROWAVE OVEN

- Prevent spilled birdseed from sprouting into weeds under the feeder. Before you put it into the feeder, microwave the birdseed 2 minutes per pound at high power. Or oven bake seeds by spreading them evenly on a cookie sheet at 250° for 30 minutes.

- Soften hard brown sugar quickly. Keep the hardened sugar in its plastic packing, add a few drops of water to the bag, and heat on medium for 20 seconds or until softened.

- Bring eggs to room temperature for baking. Put them in a small dish and heat for 10 seconds on 30% power.

- Melt chocolate easily. For 1-oz., set the power to 50%, and run the microwave for 1 to 1 1/2 minutes, then stir. Continue, and then add about 1/2 minute for each additional ounce until chocolate is fully melted. Add approximately 1 more minute for 4-oz. of chocolate.

- Melt crystallized honey. Remove the lid, then heat the jar on medium power for 30 seconds to 1 minute.

- Toast small amounts of nuts, breadcrumbs and coconut quickly. Stir in about 1/2 t. of oil to 1/4 c., spread the mixture on a plate, microwave on high for 2 to 3 minutes. Stop and stir every minute or it will burn. Ingredients may not brown. You'll know they're done by the smell.

- Get the most juice from a lemon or lime. Microwave it for 30 seconds before squeezing.

- Cut a fresh squash easily. Microwave it for a few minutes before you apply the knife.

- Cut cooking time for grilled vegetables. First cook them partway in the microwave—bell peppers for about 1 minute, new potatoes (after you prick them) for about 2 minutes.

- Disinfect sponges. Soak them in white vinegar or lemon juice, then microwave them for 1 minute.

- Disinfect a cutting board. Wash it well, then rub it with the cut side of a lemon and finally microwave it for 1 minute on high.

- Save double boiler cleaning up. When a recipe for homemade beauty products calls for a double boiler, use the microwave instead.

- Roast garlic. The process takes an hour in the oven, 8 minutes in the microwave. Slice off the top of the head to reveal all the cloves. Place in a small, deep microwaveable dish and drizzle with about 2 T. of good olive oil. Spoon 2 T. of water into the bottom of the dish, cover it with plastic wrap, and cook at medium power for 7 minutes. Let stand a few minutes before unwrapping.

MILK, POWDERED

- Clean your face. The lactic acid in milk does the job gently and removes dead cells, too. Apply a paste of powdered milk and water, then rinse. Put the powdered milk in a covered jar with a small scoop and use daily.

- Revive limp curtains. To the final rinse water, add 1 c. dry milk. (You can substitute 1/2 c. liquid starch, or 1 c. Epsom salts.)

- Revitalize permanent press items. Add powdered milk to the rinse water.

MILK CARTONS AND JUGS

- Double or triple your closet space. Place a plastic ring from a milk jug over the top of a hanger, then hang another clothes hanger from it.

- Make a kid's crayon carrier. The carton already has a handle. Just make a 4 x 6 hole in the jug.

- Make a portable "faucet" when camping. Poke a hole near the bottom of a plastic milk jug and plug it with a golf tee before filling with water. Place a bar of soap inside the leg of an old pair of pantyhose and tie it to the jug handle. To wash hands, loosen the cap, then remove the golf tee. Wet your hands with water, then replace the golf tee to stop the flow of water. Scrub your hands with the nylon and soap and unplug the hole to rinse hands.

- Improvise a strainer or colander. Cut off the top of a milk jug, then use an awl or an army knife to poke holes in the bottom.

- Make large blocks of ice for punch.

- Create luminaries. Cut off the top of a milk jug, then fill the bottom with two inches of sand and place a votive candle in it.

- Make an emergency dust pan. Cut off the bottom and with the handle facing up, cut the top off in angle.

- Cut the top off a jug and use it to stash orphaned socks in the laundry room. When the mate shows up it'll be easy to match up.

MILK CRATES

- Make stackable holders for books, binders, notebooks, schoolwork and records.

MILK OF MAGNESIA

- Preserve newspaper clippings. Mix together 1 qt. of club soda and 2 T. liquid milk of magnesia. Refrigerate overnight before using. Pour into a shallow pan that is large enough to lay the clipping down. Once the mixture has cooled down, place the clipping into the solution and let it set for I hour. Remove and lay between two pieces of solid white paper toweling.

- Use as a face mask for oily skin.

MINERAL OIL

- Revive wooden knife handles. Rub them with mineral oil.

MINERAL SPIRITS

- Take tree sap off a deck. Rub the stained area with mineral spirits on a clean cloth. Then wash the area with an all-purpose cleaner and rinse thoroughly.

MINER'S HEADLIGHT

- Illuminate nighttime cookouts. Wear a camping headlight or miner's light.

MINIBLIND SLATS

- Make plant markers. Cut slats into short lengths and label them with a waterproof pen.

MIRROR TILES

- Use as closet helpers. Mount mirror tiles on the ceiling and you'll know just what's on those high shelves.

MIXING BOWLS

- Improvise a double boiler. For the bottom use a stockpot, and for the top use a stainless steel mixing bowl.

- Find and remove pin bones from a fillet of salmon. Turn a mixing bowl over and lay the fillet over it, flesh side up. The curve of the bowl forces the pin bones to stick up, so they are easy to grasp with pliers and remove.

MOTHBALLS

- Absorb moisture and prevent rust in a toolbox. A dozen or so will do it.

- Repel pests. Put mothballs into a sealed container (to protect kids and pets), then punch holes in it and leave it in areas where the scent will repel spiders, raccoons, etc.

MOUNTAIN DEW

- Kill hornets. Add 1 T. of dishwashing soap to an open can of Mountain Dew and place near the wasps. The sweet soda attracts the insects. When they climb into the can for a drink, they'll get stuck and drown.

MOUSE PAD

- Keep cushions on furniture in place. Place a mouse pad under the cushion.

MOUTHWASH

- Sterilize toothbrushes. Soak them in Listerine.

- Keep the Christmas tree looking healthy. Water it regularly with 2 oz. of Listerine mouthwash mixed in 1 qt. of hot water. The antibacterial properties in the mouthwash will help keep the water free of bacteria.

- Disinfect a cut or broken blister. Mouthwash is an antiseptic.

MR. CLEAN

- Make a cleaner for silver and gold jewelry. In an 8-oz. container, like a pickle jar, combine 1/4 cup of Mr. Clean, dishwashing liquid, and ammonia. Shake well and heat the solution in a microwave. Place jewelry into solution and let sit for ten minutes. Remove from solution and rinse with water.

MUFFIN TIN

- Use to bake stuffed peppers. Add a splash of water to each cup. The peppers will stay moist and stand up straight.

- Use as a holder to bake potatoes. Skin will come out crisp.

- Cook meat loaf in a hurry. Instead of one large loaf, make several small muffin-sized ones.

MUSTARD POWDER

- Stop squirrels from eating your tulip bulbs. Sprinkle mustard powder around the bulbs as you plant them. Squirrels hate the taste.

NAIL POLISH

- Use as emergency glue.

- Use on a stamp or envelope flap that won't stick.

- Prevent wooden hangers from snagging clothes. Paint clear nail polish over rough spots.

- Keep holes in sweaters from getting bigger. Dab a bit of clear nail polish on the inside of the sweater. (Glue works, too.)

NAILS

- Make your violet plants lush. They'll sprout more flowers if a few metal nails are inserted into the soil. As the nails rust they release iron, a nutrient the violets love.

NEWSPAPER

- Make fire starters. Roll newspaper as tightly as you can into a log. Slip the roll inside a paper towel tube.

- Protect a window frame before you paint it. Wet strips of newspaper and stick the straight edge up against the frame. Paper will peel off easily.

NIGHT LIGHTS

- Add a light source. Attach a night light to an extension cord when you need more illumination.

NYLON NETTING

- Prevent a bathtub drain from clogging. Stick a tiny piece of nylon netting into the tub drain to catch hairs. Replace the netting when dirty.

- Remove excess dryer lint. Place a piece of nylon netting in your dryer load.

- Keep shower soap from getting mushy. Store it in a nylon net bag.

OIL OF CLOVES

- Deter puppies from chewing. Rub oil of cloves onto the table legs.

- Relieve toothache pain. Apply oil or chew on a whole clove.

OILS

- Remove fingerprints and smears on stainless sinks and appliances. Put some olive oil, lemon oil or baby oil on a soft, clean dry cloth and rub it on.

- Remove price labels. Saturate the label with salad oil, leave for a while, then rub off.

ONIONS

- Fake the scent of home cooking. Sauté an onion in a little oil and people may assume the take-out meal was cooked on the premises.

OVEN CLEANER

- Remove oil-based paint from fabric. Spray Easy Off on the paint spot and leave for half an hour, then wash garment as usual. Safe for polyester and cotton, even if paint is dried on.

- Remove bathroom mildew. Spray tub, shower door, even shower curtain with Easy Off, let stand five minutes, then clean up with a damp cloth.

- Remove terrible bathtub stains (even on fiberglass). Spray from the bottom up, leave for 20 minutes, then rinse.

- Clean accumulated pitch and tar off power-saw blades. Spray and leave briefly, rinse.

- Remove encrusted food from baking dishes (non-aluminum dishes only). Warm dish in oven, then spray with oven cleaner. Cool, then wash with warm soapy water.

- Remove yellow stains from clothes. Spray on oven cleaner, let set for 30 minutes and launder in hot water. A repeat application may be needed (though this won't restore fabric that has been damaged by perspiration stains).

PAINT BRUSHES

- Use to baste food. A two-inch or wider natural bristle paint brush is an ideal tool for this purpose.

- Clean a lampshade. A clean bristle paintbrush will work even on pleated shades, when most vacuum attachments will not.

- Butter the corn on the cob fast by brushing it with a new paintbrush.

PAINT ROLLER

- Make a shin protector for a ladder. Slit a paint roller, then slip it over the edge of the step to cushion your shins.

PAINT ROLLER PAN

- Pour melted butter into the ditch of a new paint roller pan and roll corn on the cob to butter quickly.

PANTY LINERS

- Protect clothing from excessive perspiration. Make under-arm shields by removing the adhesive strips from maxi pads and attaching them inside the armholes of a garment.

PANTYHOSE

- Replace a broken fan belt. The pantyhose can do in a pinch, until you get to a repair shop.

- Remove insulating material that may be clinging to your skin. Rub the area with the leg of a pair of pantyhose. The rubbing will generate static electricity and pull out the fibers.

- Make an umbrella cover. Stretch one leg over an umbrella, then tie the other leg around the handle to hold it in place. The pantyhose protects but allows the umbrella to breathe, discouraging mildew and rotting. It doesn't look pretty but it does the job.

- Keep onions from spoiling. Since they spoil faster when they touch each other, keep them separated in a clean, cut-off leg of a pair of pantyhose. Drop in one onion at a time, making a knot in between each onion, and hang the holder in the pantry. Cut below the knot to release one onion at a time.

- Make a soap holder for outdoor cleanup. Put a bar of soap into a cut-off leg of a pair of pantyhose and tie it to the outside faucet.

- Create odor-neutralizing sachets. Pour some baking soda into a cut-off pantyhose leg, then twist and tie the ends shut. Place in sneakers, hampers or anyplace else there's an odor.

- Make a leech protector for wading. Wear knee-high hose when you're going into a lake or a swamp.

- Use as a rope. Keep a pair in the trunk of your car to use as a tie-down for the trunk. It works just like a bungee cord.

- Wear over a cast. Cut off a leg and slip it over a cast. Slacks will be much easier to slip on and off.

- Apply stain. Nothing works better than pieces of pantyhose to stain hard-to-reach places.

- Tie newspapers together. Use the elastic around the waist of a pair of pantyhose as a large rubber band to tie newspaper and magazines.

- Make a plant tie. Cut hose into strips and use it to tie tomato and other plants to stakes.

- Strain paint. Stretch pantyhose over a bucket and hold it securely in place with a rubber band.

- Wash your back. Center a bar of soap inside the cut-off leg of a pair of pantyhose. Tie a knot on both sides of the soap. You now have the perfect back scrubber.

- Prepare an herbal bath. Fill a cut-off leg with favorite herbs (mint, rosemary, thyme), tie shut and let it float in the tub while you bathe. Or attach it to the bathtub faucet and let the water run through the herbs for a relaxing bath.

- Remove nail polish. Instead of cotton balls, cut pantyhose into 1-inch rings. Apply nail polish remover to your nail, wrap a ring around your nail, let set for a while, then rub off polish.

- Reduce lint in the dryer. Dry the clothing along with a pair of pantyhose. Tie a knot in the middle so the hose doesn't tangle.

- Protect your skin under an ice pack. Cover it with a few layers of pantyhose before you apply it.

PAPER

- Protect your fingers when hammering. Poke a small nail or brad through a folded piece of paper to keep it steady. Pull the paper out before the nail is driven in completely.

PAPER CLIPS

- Keep snack food bags closed.

- Keep the plastic bag from slipping down inside the garbage pail or trash basket. A binder clip is ideal.

- Use as a bookmark.

- Hold extra keys on your key chain.

- Use as a zipper pull.

- Make a chain if needed by linking them together.

- Use as ornament hangers.

PAPER PLATES

- Make disposable covers for microwave foods.

- Move furniture easily. Slip plate under each leg.

- Protect your fine china. Place paper plates between china ones.

PAPER TOWELS

- Make a liner for your produce drawers.

- Remove bacon grease. Pour the grease out of a pan, then crumple a piece of paper toweling, grab it with tongs, and use it to swab the extra grease from the pan.

PARCHMENT PAPER

- Make a banner for the birthday boy, bride-to-be, etc. When the party is over, roll it up and store in its original box.
- Make a stencil. Trace around a cookie cutter.
- Keep refrigerator cookie dough from sticking. Wrap it in parchment paper.
- Make a perfect pizza crust. Bake the pizza on parchment paper.

PASTE WAX

- Stop condensation from forming on the outside of a toilet tank. Shut off the water valve, then drain the tank. Dry the inside of the tank with a hair blower or fan. Then apply a thin coat of paste wax.

PASTRY BLENDER

- Cut up browned hamburger.
- Chop eggs for egg salad.
- Chop canned tomatoes.
- Mix meat loaf ingredients.

PEANUT BUTTER

- Remove chewing gum from hair. Rub with creamy peanut butter. (Don't use the chunky kind.) You'll be able to pull out the gum without causing pain.

PENCIL ERASERS

- Protect a table. Cut off slices from a pencil eraser and glue it to the bottom of vases or knickknacks to keep them from scratching a table surface.
- Replace an earring back.

PENS

- Store fishing sinkers. Remove the ink tube in an old ball-point pen and stow the sinkers here, then store the pen in your tackle box.

PEPPER

- Repair a slow leak in the car radiator. Dump in a can of black pepper and swirl it around. It goes to pinhole leaks, swells up and plugs the holes to prevent coolant from draining out. This fix may last for several years.

PERFUME SAMPLE

- Refresh potpourri. Sprinkle it with a perfume sample.

PETROLEUM JELLY

- Cover up your braces in a photograph. Use the trick that models use. Rub a bit of Vaseline on the braces (it'll refract the light) and rub it off afterwards.

- Prevent tools from rusting. Coat them with petroleum jelly.

- Soften an old baseball glove. Work the Vaseline into the glove, slip a ball into the glove, and use a rubber band to hold it in position around the glove.

- Unscrew outdoor light bulbs easily. Rub a light coat of Vaseline on the threads of the bulb before you screw it in.

- Remove lipstick on napkins. Rub jelly on the stained area, then launder the napkin.

- Keep nail polish cap from sticking. Coat the threads of the bottle with petroleum jelly.

- Soften your feet. Before taking a long walk, rub your feet with Vaseline and wear thick walking socks.

- Disassemble an artificial Christmas tree easily. Rub a light coating of Vaseline on the end of each branch before you insert it.

- Treat cracks in a dog's foot pad. Rub in some Vaseline.

- Make traps for house plant pests. Cut bright yellow margarine tubs into small rectangles and coat with Vaseline. Attach to a small stake and insert into a house plant to attract aphids and whiteflies.

- Remove a candle stub easily. Rub a thin coating of Vaseline on the inside of a candleholder before you use it.

- Use as a lubricant whenever oil or grease is not available.

- Remove a stuck ring from your finger. Coat the ring and finger and the ring will slide off.

- Polish patent leather shoes. Apply a dab, then buff it off with a soft cloth.

- Keep pests out of the pet food dish. Make a "moat" by putting some water into a pie plate, then place the food dish in the pie plate. Put petroleum jelly on and just under the rim of the pie plate too. The ants get stuck in it, so the food stays ant and bug-free.

- Keep pests out of the house. Locate the hole or crack they're coming through and repair it. Then, dab petroleum jelly mixed with chili powder on the repaired spots. Squirrels and other pests will stay clear, though critters from Mexico might be intrigued!

PHOTO ALBUM

- Store recipes neatly. When you slip them into the pages of a "magnetic" photo album they're easy to remove for reference and pages wipe off if food is dripped on them.

PHOTOCOPIER

- Make extra wallpaper border. A friend purchased some on closeout and came up 4 inches short at the end of the job. Someone suggested photocopying a section of the border on a good quality paper. It worked!

PICKLE JUICE (DILL)

- Spice up vegetables.

- Combine with finely shredded purple cabbage.

- Cut carrots matchstick shape and put them in dill pickle juice.

- Combine juice with fresh spears of cucumber.

- Also good for large diced pieces of celery.

PICKLE JUICE (SWEET)

- Flavor meat. Try adding juice to meatloaf.

- Tenderize and glaze pork chops. Brown them, drain off fat, and add pickle juice, cover and cool.

- Baste a ham with cloves, mustard and pickle juice.

- Combine leftover boned chicken with juice, vinegar and sugar.

- Try it on back bacon.

- Make mayo-free meat salads. Grind leftover or deli ham, cut green pepper and celery fine, then stir in some pickle relish and pickle juice.

- Marinate uncooked chicken in pickle juice plus Dijon mustard and garlic; drain, bake at 350° for 45 minutes, basting every 15 minutes.

- Make sweet and sour gravy for any meatball mixture. Mix 1-2 c. pickle juice, juice of 2 lemons, 1/4 c. chili sauce or ketchup. To thicken combine 2 T. cornstarch and 1/2 c. water, pour in, heat and stir for 5 minutes.

- Make brisket of beef. Mix pickle juice, plus a package each of onion soup mix and mushroom soup mix. Pour over brisket, cover with aluminum foil and bake at 300° for 3 hours (similar to sauerbraten gravy).

- Or, after browning roast, pour sweet pickle juice over meat, simmer for a couple of hours, covered, till done.

- Simmer deli pastrami slices in it; serve on rye with mustard.

- Marinate steak in pickle juice.

- Whip juice with cream cheese and use as a dip for vegetables.

- Use juice to make mincemeat.

- Pour down the kitchen drain to clean and keep it smelling sweet.

- Clean burned-on food off cast iron skillets. Get them hot, pour pickle juice on, simmer for 5 minutes and rinse.

- Juice cleans pots and pans with copper bottoms.

- Use in the garden: Pour pickle juice around gardenia and azalea bushes at least once a year. They love the acid in pickle juice.

PIE PLATE

- Protect a cookbook while you work. Invert a glass pie plate or other glass dish over an open cookbook so you can still read the recipe while protecting the page from spills.

PILLOWCASES

- Cover the mattress on a changing table. A king or queen-size pillowcase does the job.

- Use as a garment cover.

- Dry herbs by dropping them into an old but clean pillowcase. Hang on a clothesline for a couple of sunny days and they should be dry.

PINE-SOL

- Fake cleaning. Add 1/4 c. of Pine-sol cleaner to a spray bottle and fill it with water. Before a snoopy neighbor or critical houseguest walks in the door, spritz the place down. Everyone will think you've been scrubbing all day. (Another trick: rearrange the furniture.)

PIPE CLEANERS

- Clean anything with a small opening. Works on a clogged stove burner, squirt bottle tops, and acrylic paint bottles.

- Use as hooks for Christmas tree ornaments.

- Make substitute twist ties for bread bags.

- Tie together a bouquet of flowers.

PIZZA CUTTERS

- Cut bite-sized bits for young children. A wheel pizza cutter does the trick on pancakes, waffles and other foods.

PLACE MATS

- Line vegetable and meat drawers. They're the perfect size and easy to clean.

PLASTIC BINS

- Do hand laundry in your car. Just fill a covered plastic bin with water, detergent and the dirty clothes. Make sure the lid's on tight, then place it in the trunk. When you drive, the motion will agitate the laundry, which cleans the clothes. Rinse the same way.

- Collect soiled face and hand towels. Keep a small bin under your bathroom sink for this purpose.

PLASTIC BOTTLE CAPS

- Protect tubular aluminum furniture feet. Plastic caps from 2-liter soft drink containers will keep them from digging into the grass.

PLASTIC FOAM TRAY

- Make painting jobs easier. Push drawer pulls, screws and bolts into these trays (in which supermarket meat is packed) and you can paint them quickly rather than painstakingly. They'll be dry by the next day or so.

PLASTIC LIDS

- Keep burgers separated in the freezer. Place lids between patties when you prepare them for storage.

- Prevent rusting on the counter or in the cabinet. Set shaving cans on plastic lids.

- Use as spoon rests.

- Use under the honey container. Protect the cupboard surface from getting sticky.

- Fit onto a small flour sifter. You're not supposed to wash a sifter (since the dough will clog it up), and the lid keeps leftover flour from drifting onto the shelf.

PLASTIC SCRAPER

- Use for quick cleanups. For example, quickly scrape up a gob of jelly or peanut butter.

PLASTIC TARP

- Protect your lawn when digging a hole. Toss the dirt on a plastic tarp and drag the dirt away or store it until it's time to refill the hole.

PLASTIC WRAP

- Keep ice cream fit to eat. It won't dry out, discolor or frost over if you cover the surface with plastic wrap before putting on the lid.

- Prevent gasoline from running out of the lawn mower. It won't escape from the vent cap when you tilt it to make repairs if you place a piece of plastic wrap over the opening, then screw the cap back on. Use this tip on your chain saw too.

PLATE

- Keep a beret in shape. After you wash it, place a dinner place inside of it and let it dry thoroughly.

PLUNGER

- Get agitation action when doing a hand wash. Drill several holes in a small rubber plunger, put the clothes in a small basin, then plunge away. Clothes will be cleaner.

- Mark a skirt for hemming. Mark the handle of a sink plunger at the desired length, then move the plunger around the hem as it stands on its own.

POLAROID CAMERA

- Get a good look at your new eye glasses. Take a Polaroid camera along and ask a friend (or the salesperson) to snap you in your top choice. That's better than squinting in the mirror to see how the frames look on you.

PONYTAIL HOLDERS

- Childproof a door. Place a large plastic ball-type ponytail holder over the top hinge pin to keep doors from closing on small fingers. Holders won't damage door or frames.

POPCORN POPPER

- Prevent nuts from burning. Roast them in a hand-cranked stovetop popcorn popper.

POST-IT NOTES

- Give yourself a morning memory jog. Stick a Post-it with "Things to Do" items on your bathroom mirror.

- Keep track of leftovers. Stick a Post-it on the container with a note to "Eat by [whatever date]."

- Use as price tags for garage sales.

- Post on car windows to block sun that's getting in your eyes. It can be moved as the position of the sun changes.

- Remind yourself of what you're supposed to take from home. At eye level inside the front door, place a bright colored Post-it with items listed.

POT LID

- Protect recipe cards or a cookbook from food splatters. Cover with a clean glass pot lid. Its weight will also help keep the book open.

POT SCRUBBER

- Secure small items in the dishwasher. Put a nylon pot scrubber into the bottom of the silverware container, then use it as if it were a pin cushion and push small items into it.

POTATO

- Transport a flower cutting. Poke a small hole into a potato and insert the cutting into the hole.

- Prevent a meal from sticking to a barbecue grill. Rub the cut side of a potato on the grill and the potato juices will do the job.

- Remove a broken light bulb. First unplug the lamp or turn off the power. Cut a potato in half, push it into the broken bulb base and twist the light bulb out.

POTATO CHIP BAG

- Coat items before frying. Put items in the bag with flour, then shake them up. A potato chip bag is much sturdier than a brown bag.

POTATO CHIP CANS

- Store paint-filled rollers. Just make sure the lid is on airtight.

POTATO MASHER

- Soften frozen concentrated juice.
- Mix meatloaf quickly.

- Mark the top of peanut butter cookie dough. The potato masher makes a nice pattern much more quickly than a fork.

- Get help when hand-washing. When you wash delicate items by hand, you don't get the agitation action of a machine. However, you can simulate it with a potato masher. (It's very good for working on a stained area.)

POTATO RICER

- Use to puree squash.

- Make a batch of deviled eggs quickly. Press the yolks through a potato ricer.

PREPARATION H

- Soothe inflammation around a blister.

PUSHPINS

- Protect your paint job. Stick a pushpin into the back side of a cabinet door after painting. If anyone accidentally closes the door, it will not stick.

PUTTY

- Keep pictures hanging straight. Place a small amount of mounting putty (available at hardware stores) behind one corner of the frame.

- Prevent trays from sliding in drawers. Place putty at the bottom of the tray. (Florist's clay or poster tack works, too.)

PVC PIPE

- Use to store rubber and bungee cords. Cut a PVC pipe length slightly longer than the cords. Hook one end of cord to each end of the pipe.

RACK (DISH OR V-SHAPED ROASTING)

- Hold and protect a cookbook while you work.

- Store lids in a cabinet.

RAKE

- Straighten up a kid's room fast. Give it a swipe with a plastic leaf rake.

RAZOR

- Use a sharp safety razor (a single-edged razor in a safety holder) for heavy-duty scraping. It can scrape dried paint off a window or remove a stain on a Ceran stove top. Do not point the razor (or any scraping tool) straight down, to avoid damaging the surface underneath. Wedge the tool under whatever you're scraping off and try to lift it. Always use a lubricating medium (such as oil or water) to prevent scratches.

RICE

- Clean narrow-necked vases and decanters. Add uncooked rice to the soapy water. The rice will act as an abrasive to scrub any sediment. (A thin brush helps, too.)

- Prevent clumps in the salt shaker. Add a few grains of rice.

- Make an ice pack that conforms to your body. Fill a plastic freezer bag with rice and freeze.

RUBBER BANDS

- Keep caddy from slipping off the neck of the shower head. Wrap a fat rubber band around the neck.

- Wrap the ends of tongs with rubber bands to keep closed.

- Here's an easy way to track how much the bread dough rises. First add the dough to a large, clear container, then mark the height by placing a rubber band around the container. Now you'll be able to judge when the dough has doubled.

RUBBER MATS

- Stop sofa seat cushions from sliding. Set a thin rubber mat under the cushion or pin a hand towel on the base of the couch.

- Steady the baby in the high chair. Put a rubber sink mat on the seat so baby doesn't slip under the tray.

RUBBER SPATULA

- Protect a wall. Place a rubber spatula underneath the head of a hammer when removing a nail from a wall. No marring.

SAFETY GLASSES

- Wear safety glasses to prevent tears when chopping onions. If they don't work, try swimming goggles.

SALAD SPINNER

- Spin hand washables dry.

- Protect a frosted cake. Turn the outer bowl of a salad spinner upside down and put the cake underneath.

- Remove excess water from grated potatoes, cooked spinach, parsley, and fresh tomatoes. (Sliced tomatoes dried like this won't make your pizza soggy.) Water will be absorbed more quickly if you add a couple of sheets of paper toweling to the salad spinner.

SALT

- Defrost meats quickly. Place wrapped meat in a bowl of cool water and pour a generous amount of salt into the water and on top of the package. Cover the bowl with a lid and let stand for approximately an hour. The salt will work on frozen meat just like it does on a frozen sidewalk.

- Pick up a dropped egg. Sprinkle salt on the mess and leave it there for 20 minutes. You'll be able to wipe it right up.

- Freshen a sour sponge. Soak it in salt water overnight.

- Clean up oven spills. If food boils over, sprinkle salt on the spill to stop smoke and odor from forming. When the oven cools down it'll be easy to wipe up.

- Eliminate a grease stain on upholstery. Sprinkle liberally with salt as soon as possible. Allow the salt to absorb the grease. Remove salt and then dab with a damp cloth and dish soap. Blot and then rinse off with another clean soft cloth.

- Soothe a bee sting. Wet the sting right away, then cover it with salt

- Clean a cutting board. Cover it with bleach and salt, scrub it with a stiff brush, then rinse with very hot water and wipe with a clean cloth.

- Clean the brown spots (from starch) off a non-stick sole plate (the bottom of your iron). Sprinkle salt on a sheet of waxed paper, slide the iron across it, then rub lightly with silver polish.

- Kill grass growing in cracks in the cement or between patio stones. Sprinkle salt on the grass and pour very hot water over it. Or sprinkle coarse salt on the grass, let stand all day or overnight, then pour hot tap water over it.

- Keep sliced potatoes and apples from turning brown. Put them in salted cold water.

- Clean silk flowers. Put them in a bag of coarse salt and shake the bag. Take a look at the color of the salt and you'll see what you've accomplished.

- Clean coffee or tea stains from china cups. Rub them with salt.

- Clean tarnished copper. Fill a 16-oz. spray bottle with hot white vinegar and 3 T. of salt. Spray it onto the copper, let it set briefly, then rub clean. (Don't try this on lacquered copper.)

- Clean a glass coffeepot. Fill it with 1/4 c. of table salt and a dozen ice cubes. Swish the mixture around, let it sit for half an hour, then fill it with cold water and rinse.

- Halt an overflowing washing machine. Sprinkle salt on the top of the suds.

- Relieve a sore throat. Gargle with warm salt water.

- Hasten the healing of inflamed gum tissue. Rinse your mouth out with salt water several times a day.

SANDPAPER

- Fix a sticky door. If the door is sticking on a high spot, tape a piece of rough sandpaper underneath. In a few days, normal usage will have done the sanding for you.

- Open a jar. Use a sheet of fine grit sandpaper. Hold the lid with the sandpaper, grit side down, and twist the lid off.

- Make new shoes safer. Rub sandpaper on soles to avoid slipping. (Or rub the new shoes over sidewalk pavement.)

- Remove scuff marks on suede shoes. Use very fine sandpaper.

SCARF

- Protect your hairdo when you dress. Place a silk scarf over your head, then gently slip the garment over your head.

SCISSORS

- Use as an all-purpose kitchen tool. Cut pizza, dice meat, trim string beans, snip vegetables and flowers.

SCRATCH-AND-SNIFF FRAGRANCE SAMPLES

- Tuck into the cushions of your living room furniture.

- Put in your lingerie drawers.

SCRUBBING BUBBLES

- Clean vinyl tennis shoes. Spray it on and let set for a few minutes. It'll really make them really white again.

- Remove difficult siding stains. Spray it on and wash off stains and dirt.

- Take it camping. You'll be prepared for any dirty toilet seat you encounter.

SEAM RIPPER

- Open snow peas.

- Remove vein from shrimp.

SELF-ADHESIVE LABELS

- Make postcard-writing easy. Before you leave on vacation, write down names and addresses on self-adhesive labels.

SHAVING CREAM

- Prevent bathroom mirrors from fogging. Smear the mirror with a non-gel shaving cream like Barbasol, then wipe it off with a clean dry cloth. Reapply occasionally.

- Clean greasy hands. Squirt Barbasol in one hand, sprinkle sugar on the other, rub briskly and wash.

- Remove stains from carpeting.

- Clean dirty white canvas tennis shoes. Spray on Barbasol, let it set for a while, then scrub with a soft brush and toss them into the machine. Wash on the gentle cycle and add fabric softener to the rinse water. Hang to dry.

SHOE ORGANIZER

- Store your bills. Most organizers come with 12 compartments for 6 pairs of shoes. Designate one pocket for each month of the year.

- Stow bathroom supplies. Hang a shoe organizer on the bathroom door for this purpose.

- Store spray cans of paint in your workshop.

- Store baby's products. Hang a shoe organizer behind the changing table.

- Display and organize toys. Good for small dolls, stuffed animals and accessories.

SHOP VAC

- Suck up bugs in the garden, patio or sidewalk. Make sure soapy water is in the canister so the bugs don't escape.

SHOWER CAPS

- Use as shoe coverups. When you interrupt your outdoor gardening to go inside to take a call or get a drink, you won't have to worry about tracking dirt inside if you have caps handy near the door.

SHOWER CURTAIN

- Use it as a tarp. Store the shower curtain (or an old tablecloth) in the car trunk to use when hauling messy items or to kneel on if you have car trouble.

- Protect the floor under the high chair.

- Use it to haul leaves to the compost pile.

SILICA GEL PACKETS

- Keep storage boxes moisture-free. Use them in tool boxes, for example.

- Keep meringues crisp. Place a packet in a container holding meringues shells or decorations.

SILICONE SPRAY

- Slip tight boots on easily. Spray the inside with silicone spray.

SILK FLOWERS

- Fill in the garden. When your violets are in a slump, just add artificial blossoms to the sick plant and it will look good as new!

SILLY PUTTY

- Make an ear plug. My husband snores and I've tried every type of ear plug on the market. This works best. Make small balls about the size of a nickel and place them over the opening of your ears.

SKI

- Make it into a shelf. Turn an old ski upside down and set it on brackets

SLOTTED SPOON

- Measure the temperature of cooking oil. Slip a thin-stemmed, instant-read cooking thermometer through a slotted spoon.

SOAP

- Store sewing needles and pins in a bar of soap. They'll slide through fabric more easily too.

SOAP SLIVERS

- Make liquid soap. Collect the slivers in a jar, add water, then blend in a blender.

- Make a soap-filled scrubber. Sew a washcloth into a bag, stuff the slivers inside, and scrub away.

- Have a handy outdoor clean-up station. Place slivers in a pantyhose leg and tie it to the outdoor water faucet. Or hang the leg in the shower as soap on a rope.

- Keep your screws and bolts in good shape. Add soap slivers to the jars in which you keep them; it slows corrosion and lubricates the threads.

- Make sachets for dresser drawers.

- Make leg-shaving foam. Put soap slivers in a mug and add a little water. Lather with shaving brush and apply.

- Do a quick toilet cleanup. Drop a sliver in the bowl at night, leave till morning: then swish the bowl with a brush.

SOCKS

- Clean the baseboards. When you vacuum, wear an old pair of socks. Rather than bend down, wipe your feet along the baseboard, then vacuum.

- Make a door snake to prevent drafts. Fill a long sock with sand and stitch the end closed. Place at the bottom of the door to prevent air from seeping inside.

- Eliminate marred floors when moving furniture. Slip old heavy socks over the legs.

- Keep shirtsleeves pushed up. Cut strips off the top of a crew sock and slip them over your shirtsleeves to make perfect garters. When you push the sleeves up, they'll stay put.

- Use as shoe covers when you travel.

- Paint or stain stair spindles or chair rungs quickly. Slip a plastic bag over your hand and then put an old clean white sock over the bag. Dip the covered hand into the paint and apply the paint by moving your hand up and down.

- Protect your forehead during a hair treatment. Wind a doubled-over tube sock around your forehead and fasten it with clothespin or another non-magnetic clip. It'll catch drips.

SODA POP PULL TAB

- Use it as a bubble blower. Dip it into a glass full of thick dishwashing detergent.

SOFT DRINK COZIES

- Prevent rust marks in the medicine cabinet. Slip the shaving cream can into a cozy.

SOFT SCRUB

- Remove a tough stain on a porcelain doll. Dab a little bleach-free Soft Scrub on a soft clean cloth.

SPADE

- Use it as a handy sprinkler stand.

SPONGES

- Use one as a spoon rest or soap dish.

- Store one in the freezer to make an ice pack.

- Use as a lint remover on clothing and furniture. Dampen the sponge first.

- Soak up drips in the umbrella stand. Place a sponge in the bottom.

- Paint with sponges. Apply stain or paint.

- Protect the wall when removing nails. Place a sponge underneath the head of the hammer.

- Make emergency kneepads. Simply duct-tape the sponges to your knees.

SPOONS

- Remove garlic and onion odors from your hands. Hold a stainless steel spoon with all five fingers. Then run cold water over your hand. The smell disappears in seconds.

- Make a warning system to prevent burned pots. Drop a metal spoon or jar lid in the bottom of a double boiler. If the spoon begins to rattle, you'll know the pot is dry.

- Lift the lid without a hot pad. Stick the end of a wooden spoon through the handle and lift.

- Protect sink from hot pots. Lay several wooden spoons on the bottom of the sink before you set down the pot.

SPRAY MOUNT

- Keep a throw rug in place. Give it two or three squirts of Spray Mount (available at office supply stores).

STEAMER BASKET

- Remove excess water from cooked spinach. Squeeze it in a collapsible vegetable steamer basket.

- Use as an emergency strainer.

STEEL WOOL PAD

- Clean rusty medicine cabinets. Use a soap-filled steel wool pad or a commercial rust-removing product.

- Get white tennis shoes white again. Clean with a damp-ened steel wool pad.

- Clean a curling iron. Unplug it, then scrub with a pad.

STRAWS

- Deal with flowers that are too short or too saggy. Add extra length or perk them up by inserting the stems into drinking straws.

- Prevent a necklace from becoming tangled. Store it in a drinking straw. Run one end through so the ends meet and fasten the necklace clasp.

- Keep clogs out of a tube of caulking. Insert a straw into the tip before you store it.

STYROFOAM CUP

- Identify an unknown carpet stain. Mist warm water onto the stain and cover with a Styrofoam cup. Let stand for approximately 30 seconds and then remove the cup. An odor from the staining material should be detected in the cup. Then use appropriate stain remover.

SUCTION CUPS

- Keep window blind cords out of the reach of children. Attach suction cups with hooks to the upper window panes, then loop the dangling cords over the hooks.

SUGAR

- Clean dirty hands quickly. Add some sugar to the soap lather and scrub.

- Deodorize your luggage. Sugar is a natural odor absorber and has no odor of its own. Drop a couple of sugar cubes in your luggage before storing so it's nice and fresh-smelling for your next trip.

- Make old-fashioned starch for doilies. Boil 1 c. super-fine sugar in 1/3 c. of water for 2 minutes. Immerse the doily into the solution and let it drip dry. (No super-fine sugar? Put the sugar in a blender and run until it is fine.)

TABASCO SAUCE

- Keep cats off the furniture. Wipe a furniture leg with chili or Tabasco sauce and blot thoroughly. You can't smell it—but the cat can.

TABLECLOTH

- Protect the floor. Put an old vinyl tablecloth under a highchair to catch food and spills.

TACKS

- Keep chair legs from sticking to newspaper when you paint. Put a small tack in the bottom of each leg to raise it slightly above the ground so it won't stick to the newspaper.

TALCUM POWDER (see BABY POWDER)

- Untangle a chain necklace. Dust the necklace with talcum powder, then use a safety pin to loosen knots.

- Keep feet dry and comfortable: Sprinkle talcum powder into each shoe, especially on a hot day.

- Help rubber gloves slip on and off easier. Dust the insides of the gloves with talc.

- Absorb a grease stain on carpeting. Sprinkle talcum powder on the stain, then gently rub the talc into the carpet and vacuum.

- Dry-wash your hair.

- Prevent friction burns when shaving with an electric shaver. Sprinkle skin with talc before shaving.

TAPE

- Tighten a loose lipstick cover. Wrap tape around the base and it won't keep slipping off.

TAPE, DOUBLE-STICK

- Organize beads for stringing. Place double-stick tape on a hard surface and place the beads or pearls in their correct order on the tape.

- Keep tiny parts in order for reassembly. When you take equipment apart, line up the pieces on double-stick tape that you've placed on a hard surface.

TAPE, ELECTRIC

- Stop the flashing VCR clock. Cover that pesky 12:00... 12:00...12:00...with a patch of black electric tape.

- ID your luggage. Use a distinctive shape or color or pattern to stick on the bag or wrap round the handle so you'll spot it faster at the baggage claim.

TAPE, MASKING

- Storing pictures. Keep track of the hooks by taping them to the back of the picture as soon as it comes off of the wall. This will also save you time when you rehang.

TAPE, PACKING

- Repair torn rings in a shower curtain. Put a piece of tape on either side of the hole, then make a new hole in the tape with a hole punch.

TELEPHONE CORD

- Organize your wiring. Cut the coiled cord off an old telephone and use the cord to wrap the wires behind a computer or stereo and keep them organized.

TENNIS BALLS

- Park correctly in the garage. Suspend a tennis ball from the garage ceiling so that it just touches the windshield when you're positioned in the right spot. You won't be rear-ended by the garage door.

- Guard against falling dust when drilling overhead. Cut a tennis ball in half, drill a hole in the center and push the drill through the hole.

- Protect baby from sharp corners on tables or other furniture. Cover the dangerous spots with tennis balls that have been cut in half or in quarters. Tape on with packing tape.

- Give yourself a foot massage. Roll your bare foot over a tennis ball for a few minutes.

- Wrap sandpaper around a tennis ball to make sanding much easier.

TERRA-COTTA POTS

- Store your kitchen equipment. Place a small pot on your kitchen sink to collect brushes, bar of soap, soap pads, etc.

THIMBLES

- Grate cheese quickly and safely. Wear a thimble on each finger to prevent cuts from the grater.

THREE-RING BINDER

- Store the kids' art collection. Buy a hole punch and a very thick 3-ring binder and keep the drawings in one place.

THUMBTACKS

- Mark where the nail should go when hanging artwork. Insert a thumbtack through a piece of duct tape, then tape it to the back of the frame, as close as possible to the wire or hanger. Hold the art against the wall in its desired location and press lightly. The thumbtack will leave a mark where the nail should go.

- Keep a picture frame in place. Place a piece of folded masking tape (sticky side up) on the bottom two corners of the picture. Stick thumbtacks through the masking tape. The tacks will prevent the frame from shifting.

TISSUE BOX

- Store used fabric softener sheets.

TOILET PAPER

- Use to start tiny seeds. Since they're hard to see on black soil, it's hard to spread them properly. Put a layer of toilet paper over the soil, then scatter the seeds on top of the paper and make sure they're distributed evenly. Sprinkle a thin layer of potting soil on top and water thoroughly. Eventually the toilet paper will dissolve. *(You won't grow toilet paper plants.)*

- Use as long-lasting and inexpensive bathroom tissue. Place a boutique-size tissue box cover over a roll of good quality toilet paper and thread the end of the roll through the slot on top.

TONGS

- Use as a garden tool. Great for jobs like picking up slugs.

TOOTHBRUSH

- Recycle the old ones for cleaning jobs. Scrub the grouting, polish the silver, rub away a stain on a garment.

- Use as a nail-grooming tool. Remove stubborn dirt with an old electric toothbrush.

TOOTHBRUSH HOLDER

- Use to hold a paring knife. Stash it in your lunch box.

TOOTHPASTE (NON-GEL)

- Remove a Kool-Aid moustache from a child's face.

- Remove white water rings from finished (not bare) wood furniture. Mix equal parts Bon Ami or baking soda and toothpaste. Dip a slightly damp, clean soft cloth into the paste. Rubbing with the grain of the wood, gently buff the marks for a few minutes. Wipe area clean, and buff to shine. Finish with a little furniture polish.

- Remove scratches on glassware.

- Wipe away scuff marks on shoes or floors.

- Eliminate ink spots on clothing. Apply toothpaste with a damp clean cloth and rub.

- Erase crayon from washable painted walls. Use toothpaste and a soft brush.

- Shine silver or gold jewelry. Polish with white toothpaste and rinse thoroughly with warm water.

- Fill small nail holes in walls. Use a dab of white toothpaste, and let it dry before you paint.

- Remove tar from skin. Rub with toothpaste on a clean cloth.

- Scrub your hands clean. Toothpaste is abrasive and is good for removing odors.

- Use as an instant spot remover. Dab off a food stain, rub in some toothpaste with a damp cloth, then wipe with a second clean damp cloth.

- Clean off bird droppings with a dollop of toothpaste and a toothbrush.

TOOTHPICK

- Fix a hole in a garden hose. Insert a toothpick, break it off, and turn on the water. The water will cause the toothpick to swell, plugging up the hole.

- Hang a picture straight. Wrap a toothpick with masking tape, sticky side out. Press against the bottom of the frame. Straighten the picture and press the frame against the wall. The picture will hang straight.

- Use as a glue applicator. Good when you want to apply just a tiny amount.

- Decorate a cake. Draw a design with a toothpick on the top of a frosted cake and then trace over with decorative frosting.

- Serve the meat to order. Use colored toothpicks to identify medium rare, medium or well-done hamburgers and steaks.

- Mark the end of the tape. If you place a toothpick at the end of the roll, you'll find the end quickly when you next need tape.

- Keep the bread from falling into the toaster. Insert a toothpick into the top portion of a small piece, like an English muffin.

- Make the garlic clove easy to retrieve from a marinade. Stick a toothpick into the clove before you toss it in.

- Rehang a picture easily. Stick a toothpick into the nail hole, then paint. When the paint is dry, remove the toothpick and rehang the picture.

TOWELS

- Protect china and crystal. Lay a thick towel in the sink before you start to wash china and crystal.

- Keep the mixing bowl steady. Place a damp towel underneath and it won't slide.

- Make quick and easy bathroom curtains. Use two hand towels for windows and beach towels for the shower.

- Clean oven racks and grills easily. Soak old towels in a solution of ammonia and hot water and place over racks in a well-ventilated room. In a few hours, rinse.

- Make a neat job of ironing embroidery. Place a white clean bath towel on the ironing board and iron the embroidered item face down on the towel.

TOY TRUCK

- When the kids have given it up as a suitable amusement, turn it into a serving piece for hard candy.

- Or stash coins in it.

TRASH CAN

- Stretch a tight pair of jeans. Slip a wet pair over the bottom of a clean trash can and leave them there until they're dry.

- Store linens and out-of-season clothing. A 40-gallon can may double as a decorators table. Just add a round plywood top, cover the can with a table skirt and top it off with a glass tabletop (both available at home stores).

TRASH CAN LID

- Make an instant pond for the garden. Turn the lid upside down and bury it in the ground up to the rim. Place pebbles inside, and fill with water.

TWIST TIES

- Keep cords organized. Group them together with twist ties.

- Make a loose screw fit. Stick a piece of a twist tie into the hole, then replace the screw in the hole.

- Use as an emergency latch.

- Fasten Christmas ornaments onto a tree.

- Reattach a button. Keep a few bread twist ties in your purse for this purpose. This works with sweaters that are loosely knit, since the fabric will not be damaged. Push the wire through the button holes and twist closed on the inside.

UMBRELLA

- Use as a drip catcher under a hanging plant. Hang an umbrella from the pot.

- Keep car seats cool. Place an umbrella over the steering wheel or car seat.

- Make chandelier cleaning a snap. Hang an umbrella upside down from the chandelier, then spray the chandelier with a cleaner containing ammonia or your own mix of 1 part alcohol to 3 parts water in a spray bottle. Let liquid collect in the umbrella.

- Make a clothesline. Strip off the cover, then attach the handle to a sturdy support on the ceiling. Hang wet clothes on a hanger before you hang them on the umbrella.

VANILLA BEAN

- Make flavored sugar. Add a slit open bean to the sugar bowl.

- Jazz up the cake. Scrape the insides of one or two beans into the cake mix or into the milk used for icing. This will make your cake taste even better.

- Keep the moths away. Put a couple of beans in the closet (in a plastic bag with holes punched in it).

- Perfume the room. Hide a few opened beans throughout a room.

VEGETABLE PEELER

- Peel slices of butter when it's hard.

- Use to substitute for a Philip's screwdriver.

- Sharpen crayons beautifully.

- Use to pit cherries.

- Make paper-thin slices of Parmesan cheese.

VELCRO

- Resize a too-big hat. Put a strip of Velcro inside the brim. This is great for little kids who like to wear cowboy and fireman hats.

- Protect the floor from scratches. Use the pile side on the bottom of dining room chair legs.

- Keep belt from slipping. Attach Velcro to the type of belt that just slips through the buckle, at the point where it's a comfortable fit.

- Balance a top-heavy vase. Attach Velcro to the vase and to the stand.

- Keep track of the remote. Put a strip of Velcro on the bottom, another on the arm of your favorite TV watching chair.

- Stop the attacks of the shower curtain. Attach a small piece of Velcro to the hemmed side of the curtain and a companion piece to the wall of the shower or tub.

VICKS VAPORUB

- Block unpleasant odors. Next time you have a smelly job to do, rub some Vicks on the top of your lip before you start. Its smell prevents you from noticing others.

VINYL RECORDS

- Make them into dip dishes. On a cookie sheet, set a record on an inverted ovenproof bowl and place in a 300° oven for 2-4 minutes. Remove with tongs and immediately place inside another bowl and shape the edges with your hands. It'll harden in a few minutes.

WADING POOLS

- Use as a beverage cooler for picnics.

- Clean window screens. Submerge them in water with a few added squirts of dishwashing detergent.

WASHCLOTHS

- Use as napkins for a messy meal.

WASHING MACHINE

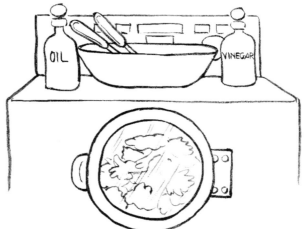

- Dry lettuce for a crowd. Wash it first, then stick it into a pillow case or mesh bag and put them into the washing machine on the "final spin" cycle.

- Clean a mildewed rubber bathmat. Toss into the washing machine, along with a load to which you're adding chlorine bleach. Air dry—in the sun, if possible.

WATER

- Prevent clogged drains. Pour boiling water down your kitchen drain a few times a month.

- Speed-dry a manicure. Dip your fingertips into a container of ice water. Be sure not to touch the sides of the bowl.

- Anchor wobbly candles. Pour hot water into the candle-holder and let it set for a few minutes. Once the holder is heated, pour out the water and fit in the candles.

- Remove wrinkles from clothing. Hang clothes on the shower curtain pole in a bathroom and fill the bathtub with the hottest water possible. Make sure the bathroom door is closed so no steam escapes. Make sure clothes are hung securely or they might fall into the tub.

WATER GLASS

- Keep a snappy curve on a baseball hat. Bend the brim and place it in an empty water glass.

WATERING CAN

- Make a twine dispenser and recycle a leaky watering can. Remove the watering head, place a ball of twine inside, and draw the twine through the spout.

WAXED PAPER

- Prevent iron skillets from rusting. Rub them with waxed paper before you put them away.

- Keep frozen hamburgers and chops from sticking together. Place a piece of waxed paper in-between hamburger patties or chops before you put them in a freezer bag.

- Clean a sticky waffle iron. Place two sheets of waxed paper into the waffle iron and heat until the paper gets dark brown. Remove the burnt paper and use as usual.

- Make defrosting easier. Layer a few pieces of wax paper on a newly defrosted freezer shelf. Next time you defrost, ice will come right off.

- Keep the ice cream from developing crystals. Press a piece of wax paper on top of an opened container, under he lid.

- Keep a slide slippery. Rub waxed paper over the surface.

- Keep hangers gliding over a clothes closet rod. Rub waxed paper over it.

- Give floor a quick shine. Place waxed paper on a mop head.

WD-40

- Remove melted crayon and lipstick from the dryer. Spray the stained area with WD-40. Wipe out the dryer with a clean cloth until the melted stuff is gone, then clean up with an all-purpose cleaner.

- Remove tar from the car. Give it a shot of WD-40.

- Prevent car lock from freezing in cold weather. Give it a spritz of WD-40.

- Remove stickers and adhesives from glass.

- Loosen stuck light bulbs. Unplug light fixture before hand.

- Remove gum from clothing.

- Slip a tight ring off finger.

- Help boots resist mud. Give them a spray of WD-40.

- Release buttons on a phone or calculator. Spray on a hit of WD-40 and they won't stick.

- Empty a wasp nest. Once you spray it with WD-40, the wasps will either take off or die, so you can tear down the nest.

WHEELBARROW

- Make a makeshift barbecue grill. Recycle an old wheelbarrow for this purpose.

- Fill with ice and use as a cooler. (You may need to line it with plastic.)

- Use as a planter. You can move it from sun to shade as necessary.

WINDEX GLASS CLEANER

- Kill wasps immediately.

- Spot clean a carpet. Test for colorfastness first.

WINDSHIELD WASHER SOLUTION

- Keep a sponge from sticking to the freezer as you clean. Sprinkle it with windshield washer solution.

WOK

- Use as a popcorn popper. Popcorn will pop evenly and there'll be less burnt kernels.

- Use as a deep fryer.

WOOLITE UPHOLSTERY CLEANER

- Clean stuffed animals that aren't machine-washable. Clean small sections at a time, being careful not to get it too wet. You'll be amazed at the results. This method can be used on expensive vintage Steiff animals. Not recommended for toys a child may put in his/her mouth.

WRENCH

- Carry a heavy bucket. Slip an open-ended wrench under the handle to distribute the weight more evenly.

YOGURT CONTAINERS

- Leave clean containers in canisters as measuring cups. A 4-oz. size yields 1/2 c., 6-oz. size yields 2/3 c. and an 8-oz. size yields 1 c.

ZEST SOAP

- Save time removing soap scum from your shower. Zest soap doesn't cause as much residue as other soaps.

TRADEMARK INFORMATION

Alka-Seltzer is a registered trademark of Miles, Inc.

Aqua Net, Q-Tips and **Vaseline** are registered trademarks of Chesebrough-Pond's USA.

Band-Aid is a registered trademark of Johnson & Johnson.

Bar Keepers Friend is a registered trademark of SerVaas Laboratories.

Barbasol is a registered trademark of Pfizer, Inc. Pfizer, Inc. does not recommend or endorse any use of Barbarsol Shaving Cream beyond those indicated on the usage instructions on the package label.

BIC is a registered trademark of BIC Corporation.

Bon Ami is a registered trademark of the Faultless Starch/Bon Ami Co.

Coca Cola is a registered trademark of the Coca Cola Company. The Coca Cola Company does not endorse any use of Coca Cola other than as a soft drink.

ChapStick is a registered trademark of A.H. Robbins Company.

Comet, Cascade, Crest, Crisco, Febreze, Ivory, Vicks, & Vapor Rub, Tide and **Zest** are registered trademarks of Proctor & Gamble.

Clorox, Mr. Clean, Pine-Sol, Soft Scrub, SOS are registered trademarks of the Clorox Company.

Crayola and **Silly Putty** are registered trademarks of Binney & Smith, Inc

Dial Liquid and **20 Mule Team** are registered trademarks of Dial Corp.

Easy Off, Jet-Dry, Lysol and **Woolite** are registered trademarks of Reckitt Benckiser.

Elmer's Glue-All is a registered trademark of Borden, Inc.

Hefty is a registered trademark of the Pactiv Corporation.

Irish Spring is a registered trademark of Colgate-Palmolive Co.

Kool-Aid is a registered trademark of Kraft Foods, Inc.

Knox is a registered trademark of NBTY, Inc., used by Kraft Foods under license.

Krazy is a registered trademark of Borden, Inc. Elmer's Products, Inc. accepts no liability for any mentioned use for Krazy Glue that is not specifically endorsed in the products packaging and labeling.

Listerine is a registered trademark of Warner-Lambert Co.

Mouli is a registered trademark of Groupe SEB.

Mountain Dew is a registered trademark of Pepsi-Cola Company

Pam is a registered trademark of International Home Foods, Inc. International Home Foods, Inc. does not endorse any use of Pam No Stick Cooking Spray other than those indicated on the label.

Playtex is registered trademark of Playtex Products, Inc.

Polaroid is a registered trademark of Polaroid Company.

Popsicle is a registered trademark of Unilever Corporation.

Post-It Notes, Scotch and **Spray Mount** are registered trademarks of 3M Company

Preparation H is a registered trademark of Whitehall-Robbins.

Purell is a registered trademark of Gojo Industries, Inc.

Reynolds Wrap is a registered trademark of Reynolds Metal Company

Rit is a registered trademark of Best Foods Company.

Scrubbing Bubbles and **Windex** are registered trademarks of S.C. Johnson & Son Inc.

Shaklee's Basic H is a registered trademark of the Shaklee Corp.

Styrofoam is a registered trademark of the Dow Chemical Company.

Tabasco is a registered trademark of McIlhenny Company.

Velcro is a registered trademark of Velcro Industries.

WD-40 is a registered trademark of WD-40 Company.

Ziploc is a registered trademark of DowBrands.

If you love tips as much as I do, send me one of your all-time favorites. If I use it in any of our publications, I'll send you a free book. In the event of duplication (and there are sure to be many), the book will go to the person whose hint I open first.
I'm looking forward to hearing from you.

Mary Ellen

Send your tips to:

Pinkham Publishing
Box 10
Grand Rapids, MN 55744

Or email me at:

m.ellen@bitstream.net